Uniform System of Financial Reporting for Spas

Uniform System of Financial Reporting for Spas

International SPA Association
Lexington, Kentucky

Educational Institute
American Hotel & Lodging Association
Orlando, Florida

Disclaimer

This publication is designed to provide accurate and authoritative information in regard to the subject matter covered. It is sold with the understanding that the publisher is not engaged in rendering legal, accounting, or other professional service. If legal advice or other expert assistance is required, the services of a competent professional person should be sought.

—*From the Declaration of Principles jointly adopted by the American Bar Association and a Committee of Publishers and Associations.*

Nothing contained in this publication shall constitute a standard, an endorsement, or a recommendation of the Educational Institute or the American Hotel & Lodging Association (AH&LA). The Institute and AH&LA disclaim any liability with respect to the use of any information, procedure, or product, or reliance thereon by any member of the hospitality industry.

2113 N. High Street
Lansing, Michigan 48906

Printed in the United States of America
2 3 4 5 6 7 8 9 10 10 09 08 07 06

ISBN 0-86612-264-8

A few words from the sponsor of this edition of the *Uniform System of Financial Reporting for Spas*

Based in Austin, Texas, HFTP is the professional association for financial and technology personnel working in hotels, resorts, clubs, casinos, restaurants and other hospitality-related businesses. The association provides continuing education and networking opportunities to more than 4,000 members around the world, and produces the premiere hospitality technology shows HITEC and ONHTEC. HFTP also administers the examination and awards the certification for the Certified Hospitality Accountant Executive (CHAE) and the Certified Hospitality Technology Professional (CHTP) designations. HFTP was founded in 1952 as the National Association of Hotel Accountants.

Contents

Preface

The International SPA Association Foundation is the 501(c)3 foundation of the International SPA Association and was created in 1999 to serve the educational and research needs of the spa industry. The ISPA Foundation's mission is to improve and enhance the value of the spa experience; its vision is to advance spa culture to sustain health and well-being. The ISPA Foundation's objectives include being the educational source for the spa industry, establishing definitive research that validates spa industry related topics and creating an endowment that sustains the ISPA Foundation in perpetuity.

In 2003, the ISPA Foundation assembled a committee to develop a uniform system of financial reporting in order to establish a standardized accounting system. This standardization will allow for informed comparisons between spas and accurate analysis of the spa industry by financial institutions. *Uniform System of Financial Reporting for Spas* provides the structure for the preparation and presentation of financial data in a consistent format, as well as a chart of accounts prepared in common industry language. Though uniform, the system has the flexibility to allow both large and small spa operations, as well as all spa types, to use the same reporting system.

Uniform System of Financial Reporting for Spas represents the first successful, organized effort to establish a definitive uniform accounting system for the spa industry. The responsibility of this task is significant and the committee members were carefully chosen to lead this monumental effort. The committee comprised professionals representing spas that range in size and scope of operations, veteran spa consultants, spa industry partners, and members of the auditing profession. In addition, a peer review of the material was conducted utilizing another diverse group of spa professionals.

The ISPA Foundation is grateful to John Korpi for leading this undertaking and for the critical role he played in the development of the system. The ISPA Foundation thanks and commends him and the committee for sharing their knowledge and expertise and their untiring devotion to the completion of this task. The committee members responsible for this inaugural edition are:

Sharilyn Abbajay, Owner, S.P. Abbajay & Associates

Andrew A. "Skip" Ariansen, Controller, Red Mountain Spa

Billy Brewer, Audit Partner, PricewaterhouseCoopers LLP

Joel Friedman, Founder and former President and V.P Sales & Marketing for "SpaSoft" Spa Scheduling and Management Software

Ann Duliere, Director of Financial Services, Golden Door

Kirsten Glerum, Director of Finance, The Ritz-Carlton Lodge, Reynolds Plantation

John Korpi, President, International SPA Association Foundation

Amy M. Martin, CPA, Partner, Calvin Martin & Company, PLLC

Jack Morrison, CMA, Managing Director, Elmcrest College of Applied Health Sciences & Spa Management

Edwin H. Neill III, CFO, Neill Corporation

Judith L. Singer, Ed.D., President & Co-Owner, Health Fitness Dynamics, Inc.

Don Walton, CHAE, CHTP, Past President, Hospitality Financial and Technology Professionals

Frank I. Wolfe, CAE, Executive Vice President & CEO, Hospitality Financial and Technology Professionals

The ISPA Foundation is honored and grateful to have worked with Ray Schmidgall, Ph.D., CPA, as the author of this book. His experience and knowledge in accounting and hospitality have helped shape this publication into the valuable resource it is.

This book would not have been possible without the support, vision and wisdom of other important partners and resources. Several organizations played a key role in the development of the uniform system.

The International SPA Association was a key partner in the development of the *Uniform System of Financial Reporting for Spas.* ISPA is recognized worldwide as the leading professional organization and voice of the spa industry and their support of this book reinforces that position.

Hospitality Financial and Technology Professionals is the professional association for financial and technology personnel working in hotels, resorts, clubs, casinos, restaurants and other hospitality-related businesses. HFTP's sponsorship, support, and involvement in this project were vital to its development and future.

The ISPA Foundation would like to thank the Educational Institute of the American Hotel & Lodging Association for editing and publishing the book under the direction of Tim Eaton, as well as George Glazer for his continued support and enthusiasm.

Through their previous publications, the Hotel Association of New York City and the International Health, Racquet and Sportsclub Association provided tested uniform system models that helped direct and guide the development of this uniform system for the spa industry.

This *Uniform System of Financial Reporting for Spas* is a first edition. The ISPA Foundation and committee welcome feedback and look to build, in future editions, on this base text. The spa industry is young and dynamic. This text represents an important step in the health and development of the spa industry.

International SPA Association Foundation
2365 Harrodsburg Road, Ste. A325
Lexington, KY 40504 USA
1.888.651.4772 or 1.859.226.4326
ispafoundation@ispastaff.com
www.experienceispa.com

Introduction

A uniform system of financial reporting establishes standardized formats and account classifications to guide individuals in the preparation and presentation of financial statements. The recommendations set forth in this uniform system are based on a consensus of spa industry financial executives, public accounting authorities, consulting specialists, and a leading academic expert, and are consistent with generally accepted accounting principles.

The resulting standardization suggested by a uniform system of financial reporting permits internal and external users of financial statements to compare the financial position and operational performance of a particular facility to similar types of facilities in the spa industry. For new spas just opening, a uniform system serves as a turnkey accounting system that can be quickly adapted to the needs and requirements of the business.

Uniform System of Financial Reporting for Spas is divided into three parts. Part I focuses on the basic financial statements prepared for spa properties. The first four sections of Part I present the formats and explain the line items on those statements typically produced for external users. These include the Balance Sheet, the Statement of Income, the Statement of Owners' Equity, and the Statement of Cash Flows. Section 5 of Part I contains a brief discussion of notes to the financial statements.

Section 6 of Part I details the format and explains the line items for departmental statements useful in reporting and analyzing operating results. The statements provided apply to full-service spa facilities with a variety of other services and amenities. Spas should delete those schedules that do not apply to their business and adapt the suggested schedules to meet their individual needs and requirements by deleting irrelevant line items and/or adding appropriate line items. However, any changes that individual spas make to the suggested format of the uniform system should be consistent with generally accepted accounting principles. It is also recommended that spas periodically review the format of their financial statements with recognized accounting experts to ensure that their procedures and statements remain in conformity with the pronouncements of the various accounting boards.

Section 7 presents short versions of several departmental schedules that smaller spas may wish to use when they are unable to collect the information necessary to distribute revenues and expenses into the categories shown on the full schedules of Section 6.

The four sections of Part II focus on financial analysis and address the following topics:

- Financial statement formats
- Ratio analysis and statistics

- Breakeven analysis
- Budgeting and budgetary control

Part III looks at some important financial tools. Section 12 presents a sample chart of accounts. Like the statements and schedules, users may need to modify the chart to assist in the recording of financial data. Section 13 contains the expense dictionary, which is designed to help spa accounting personnel classify, in accordance with the uniform system, the numerous expense items encountered in their daily work. The expense dictionary will also help serve as a ready reference for the executive, the manager, and the purchasing agent, showing them to which account or expense group the accounting department will charge each expense item.

Finally, Section 14 contains a sample summary income statement and its supporting schedules. This sample provides an example of how all of the schedules and statements tie together, as well as how they can be modified to meet the user's needs.

Part I
Financial Statements

Section 1
Balance Sheet

The Balance Sheet reflects the financial position of an operation by revealing the assets, liabilities, and owners' equity as of a given date. Simply stated, assets represent things owned by the spa, liabilities represent the claims to the assets of outsiders, and owners' equity represents the claims of the owners to the assets of the spa.

The accounts appearing on the Balance Sheet are generally arranged in a report format. This format lists assets, liabilities, and owners' equity in a single column.

The illustration of the Balance Sheet that follows includes accounts applicable to many spas. Each line item appearing on this Balance Sheet will be explained in the pages that follow.

The number and types of accounts that appear on the balance sheets of spas will vary according to the needs and requirements of individual spas. Therefore, the accounts listed on the Balance Sheet presented here may not apply to every spa operation.

Individual companies can modify the Balance Sheet to meet their own needs and requirements, while remaining consistent with generally accepted accounting principles. Accounts of a similar nature or of small or immaterial dollar amounts can be logically grouped together. However, items of sufficient importance and materiality should always be listed separately on the Balance Sheet.

BALANCE SHEET [Report Format]

Assets

	Current Year	Prior Year
CURRENT ASSETS		
Cash and Equivalents	$	$
Short-Term Investments		
Receivables		
Accounts Receivable—Guests/Members		
Notes Receivable		
Current Maturities of Noncurrent Receivables		
Other Receivables		
Total Receivables		
Less Allowance for Doubtful Accounts		
Net Receivables		
Inventories		
Retail		
Professional		
Other		
Prepaid Expenses		
Deferred Income Taxes, Current		
Other Current Assets		
Total Current Assets		
NONCURRENT RECEIVABLES, NET OF CURRENT MATURITIES		
Owners and Officers		
Other Noncurrent Receivables		
Total Noncurrent Receivables		
INVESTMENTS		
PROPERTY AND EQUIPMENT		
Land		
Buildings		
Leaseholds and Leasehold Improvements		
Construction in Progress		
Furniture, Fixtures, and Equipment		
Total Property and Equipment		
Less Accumulated Depreciation and Amortization		
Net Property and Equipment		
OTHER ASSETS		
Security and Lease Deposits		
Loan Fees		
Intangibles		
Deferred Income Taxes, Noncurrent		
Other—Other Assets		
Total Other Assets		
TOTAL ASSETS	$	$

BALANCE SHEET [Report Format, continued]

Liabilities and Owners' Equity

	Current Year	Prior Year
CURRENT LIABILITIES		
Accounts Payable	$	
Notes Payable		
Current Portion of Long-Term Debt		
Income Taxes Payable		
Accrued Expenses		
Deferred Revenue—Gift Certificates		
Deferred Revenue—Series		
Deferred Revenue—Other		
Deferred Rent		
Advance Deposits		
Deferred Income Taxes, Current		
Other Current Liabilities		
Total Current Liabilities		
LONG-TERM DEBT, NET OF CURRENT MATURITIES		
Notes and Other Similar Liabilities		
Obligations under Capital Leases		
Owners and Officers		
Total Long-Term Debt		
DEFERRED REVENUE—NONCURRENT		
DEFERRED RENT—NONCURRENT		
DEFERRED INCOME TAXES—NONCURRENT		
OTHER LONG-TERM LIABILITIES		
OWNERS' EQUITY—one of the formats found on page 6		
TOTAL LIABILITIES AND OWNERS' EQUITY	$	$

Alternative Owners' Equity Presentations in the Balance Sheet

CORPORATION
Stockholders' Equity

	Current Year	Prior Year
____% Cumulative Preferred Stock, $ ____ par value, authorized ____ shares; issued and outstanding ____ shares	$	$
Common Stock, $____ par value, authorized ____ shares; issued and outstanding ____ shares		
Additional Paid-In Capital		
Other Comprehensive Income		
Retained Earnings		
Less: Treasury Stock, ____ shares of Common Stock, at cost	______	______
Total Stockholders' Equity	$ ______	$ ______

PARTNERSHIP
Partners' Equity

	Current Year	Prior Year
Other Comprehensive Income	$	$
General Partners		
Limited Partners	______	______
Total Partners' Equity	$ ______	$ ______

LIMITED LIABILITY COMPANY

	Current Year	Prior Year
Other Comprehensive Income	$	$
Members' Equity	______	______
	$ ______	$ ______

SOLE PROPRIETORSHIP

	Current Year	Prior Year
Other Comprehensive Income	$	$
Owner's Equity	______	______
	$ ______	$ ______

ASSETS

Current Assets

This section of the Balance Sheet refers to accounts that are to be converted to cash or used in operations within 12 months of the balance sheet date. (Noncurrent assets—such as Noncurrent Receivables, Property and Equipment, and Other Assets—refer to accounts that are *not* to be converted to cash within 12 months of the balance sheet date.) The accounts appearing under the Current Assets section of the Balance Sheet are commonly listed in the order of their liquidity.

Cash and Equivalents

This line item includes cash on hand, cash in bank accounts, and temporary cash investments with original maturities of under 90 days, such as short-term certificates of deposit.

Short-Term Investments

This line item includes debt and equity securities and other short-term investments that management intends to sell within, or that have original maturities of, 12 months or less from the balance sheet date. Notes accompanying the financial statements should disclose the basis for valuation of such securities.

Receivables

This section of current assets includes current accounts receivable such as Accounts Receivable—Guests, Notes Receivable, and others. Allowance for Doubtful Accounts records the amount of current receivables estimated to be uncollectible. This amount is subtracted from Total Receivables to provide a Net Receivables amount.

Accounts Receivable—Guests/Members. This line item includes the total amount due to the spa for membership dues, individual or group accounts direct billed to the clients, and other related fees. Accounts receivable due from owners, officers, and employees, unless minor in amount, should be listed separately on the Balance Sheet. If such amounts are not expected to be collected within 12 months of the balance sheet date, they should not be included under this line item, but should be listed separately in the noncurrent assets section of the Balance Sheet under Noncurrent Receivables.

Notes Receivable. This line item includes notes receivable that are expected to be collected within 12 months of the balance sheet date. Notes receivable from owners, officers, and employees should be listed separately on the Balance Sheet. If such notes are not expected to be collected within 12 months of the balance sheet date, they should not be included under this line item, but should be listed separately in the noncurrent assets section of the Balance Sheet under Noncurrent Receivables.

Other Receivables. This line item includes current receivables that do not relate to the line items discussed previously.

Allowance for Doubtful Accounts. This line item includes the amounts of Accounts Receivable—Guests/Members, Notes Receivable, and Other current receivables that are estimated to be uncollectible. The amounts listed should be determined on the basis of generally accepted methods such as past experience and industry trends. The balance at the end of any period should be the best estimate of receivables that will not be collected.

Inventories

This line item includes the cost of items such as professional products, retail merchandise, and food and beverage that is on hand as of the balance sheet date. Unopened packages of robes, towels, etc., if significant, should be reflected in this inventory. When inventories of Retail, Professional, and Other are significant, they should be shown separately on the Balance Sheet. The basis for valuing inventories should be disclosed in the notes to the financial statements.

Prepaid Expenses

This line item includes payments that will benefit future operating periods of the spa. These expenditures are normally charged to operations on the basis of measurable benefits. Examples of Prepaid Expenses include insurance, interest, property taxes, maintenance and service contracts, rent, and other similar items.

Deferred Income Taxes, Current

This line item represents the tax effects of temporary differences between the bases of current assets and current liabilities for financial and income tax reporting purposes. For example, if the Allowance for Doubtful Accounts is not deductible for tax purposes until such time as the debt is written off, the Allowance for Doubtful Accounts will result in a current deferred tax asset. Current Deferred Income Taxes are presented as net current assets or net current liabilities as circumstances dictate.

Other Current Assets

This line item includes other current assets that are reasonably expected to be realized in cash or consumed in the normal operating cycle of the spa within 12 months of the balance sheet date. Each item, unless minor in amount, should be listed separately on the Balance Sheet.

Noncurrent Receivables

This section of the Balance Sheet includes accounts and notes that are not expected to be collected within 12 months of the balance sheet date. Amounts due from owners and officers, unless minor in amount, should be listed separately on the Balance Sheet. If appropriate, an Allowance for Doubtful Noncurrent Receivables (noncurrent receivables that are estimated to be uncollectible) should be established using procedures described previously under Allowance for Doubtful Accounts.

Investments

This line item generally includes debt or equity securities, whether or not they are traded in recognized markets, and ownership interests that are expected to be held on a long-term basis. Investments in marketable equity securities and debt securities, where there is not the intent and ability to hold such securities to maturity, should be considered "available for sale" and reflected at market value with unrealized gains and losses being shown, net of tax effects, as a separate component of equity. Investment in debt securities where there is the intent and ability to hold such securities to maturity should be considered "held to maturity" and reflected at amortized cost. Investments in entities should be shown separately, unless insignificant. Generally accepted accounting principles require that investments in entities be accounted for in one of three ways: (1) consolidated, (2) equity method, or (3) cost method. Consolidation is required if the investor owns more than 50 percent of an entity's voting interest or if the investor participates in the majority of the entity's economic interest. Consolidation requires that 100 percent of the entity's assets, liabilities, revenues, and expenses be included in the financial statements of the investor, with appropriate amounts recorded representing the minority interests not owned by the investor. Investment in entities over which the reporting entity has the ability to exercise significant influence (generally by ownership of more than 20 percent and less than 50 percent) should be recorded using the equity method. The equity method requires the recording of the investor's share of the investee's income as revenue and an increase in the carrying value of the investment. The determination of how to account for investments in entities is a complex process and management should seek the advice of their accountants. The method of accounting for and the basis for valuing investments should be disclosed in notes to the financial statements.

Property and Equipment

This section of the Balance Sheet includes the cost of the land; buildings; leaseholds and leasehold improvements; construction in progress; and furniture, fixtures, and equipment. This section also includes similar assets under capital leases. Each asset category held under a capital lease, unless minor in amount, should be listed separately on the Balance Sheet or disclosed in notes accompanying the financial statements.

Expenditures for property and equipment should be capitalized (not expensed) when they meet the four following requirements:

1. They are for tangible items.
2. The purchased items are used in the business to generate revenue.
3. The life of the items purchased exceeds one year.
4. The expenditure is considered to be significant.

Each company needs to determine the dollar level above which all expenditures on equipment and leaseholds will be capitalized and included in Property and Equipment, and below which they will be included in supplies or repair and maintenance expenses on the Income Statement. Generally, those expenditures that are greater than a minimum amount, such as $500 in a smaller operation or $1,000 in a larger operation, should be capitalized if they increase an asset's useful life or its value. All additions to property and equipment must be depreciated over an estimated useful life. If you are uncertain as to a capitalization and depreciation policy, please seek the advice of your auditor or tax accountant.

Depreciation is a method of allocating the net cost (after reduction for expected salvage value) of the individual assets or classes of assets to operations over those assets' anticipated useful lives. There are several methods used for depreciation, including straight line, declining balance, and other variants. Under generally accepted accounting principles, the straight-line method of depreciation is preferred for financial reporting. Declining balance, where allowable, is a method of depreciation usually used for tax depreciation. The number of years chosen for the life of an asset or class of assets also varies somewhat in practice for similar items; however, the methods and the lives used should result in a reasonable allocation of the cost of the assets to operations over their useful lives.

The total Accumulated Depreciation and Amortization should appear as a line item. This amount is subtracted from the preceding line items to arrive at Net Property and Equipment. Notes accompanying the financial statements of a spa or operation should disclose the methods of depreciation and amortization.

Other Assets

This section of the Balance Sheet includes noncurrent assets not referred to by other sections of the Balance Sheet. Examples of Other Assets include Security and Lease Deposits, Loan Fees, Intangibles, and Other items.

Security and Lease Deposits

This line item includes money deposited with public utility companies (such as telephone, water, electricity, gas, etc.) and other money used for similar types of deposits. Lease deposits generally represent the first, and maybe the last, month's rent for rental properties and other equipment or furniture leased for operations.

Loan Fees

This line item includes costs relating to obtaining financing. Loan Fees are customarily amortized over the life of the related debt and include such costs as fees for accounting, underwriting, and legal services. Notes accompanying the financial statements of a spa or operation should disclose the method of amortization.

Intangibles

This line item includes assets that are generally recorded in conjunction with an acquisition of a business or individual spa, such as specifically identifiable intangibles like covenants not to compete, guest lists, and other similar assets, or goodwill. A recognized intangible asset with a finite useful life is amortized (down to its residual value, if any) over the period in which the asset is expected to contribute to the future cash flows of the entity. A recognized intangible asset with an indefinite life is not amortized. Goodwill is not amortized. All recognized intangible assets and goodwill are subject to impairment tests as required under generally accepted accounting principles. These impairment tests are complex and management should consult with their accountants as to the appropriate methods and timing of impairment testing as well as the required disclosures concerning intangible assets and goodwill in the notes accompanying the financial statements of a spa or operation.

Deferred Income Taxes, Noncurrent

This line item represents the tax effects of temporary differences between the bases of Noncurrent Assets and Noncurrent Liabilities for financial and income tax reporting purposes. For example, if a liability is accrued that will not be paid for an extended period and the expense is deductible only when paid for tax purposes, the accrual will result in a Noncurrent Deferred Income Tax asset. Noncurrent Deferred Income Taxes are presented as net noncurrent assets or net noncurrent liabilities as circumstances dictate.

Other—Other Assets

Noncurrent items that cannot be included under specific groupings such as Security and Lease Deposits, Loan Fees, and Intangibles should be shown under this caption. Cash surrender value of life insurance could be included in this classification. The nature of these items, if material, should be clearly indicated on the Balance Sheet or in the notes to the financial statements.

LIABILITIES

Current Liabilities

This section of the Balance Sheet refers to obligations of the spa at the balance sheet date that are expected to be paid within one year.

Accounts Payable

This line item includes amounts due to vendors for merchandise, services, equipment, or other purchases.

Notes Payable

This line item includes short-term notes that are due within 12 months of the balance sheet date. Notes due to banks and notes due to other creditors (including owners and officers), unless minor in amount, should be listed separately on the Balance Sheet or summarized in a footnote to the financial statements. (See Long-Term Debt below for other required disclosures.)

Current Portion of Long-Term Debt

This line item includes those items not included in notes payable such as the principal payments of long-term debt such as notes and similar liabilities, sinking fund obligations, and the principal portion of capitalized leases due within 12 months of the balance sheet date.

Income Taxes Payable

This line item includes the estimated amounts of federal, state, and city income taxes payable within 12 months of the balance sheet date.

Accrued Expenses

This line item includes expenses that are incurred before the balance sheet date but that are not due until after the balance sheet date. Examples of accrued expense items include salaries, wages, bonuses and commissions and related withholding taxes, vacation pay, interest, steam and electricity, telephone service, water, and gas. To illustrate accrued wages, consider a spa that paid its 10 employees through December 29, 20X1. These ten employees worked 150 hours on December 30–31, 20X1, and will be paid these wages on January 12, 20X2. Since the wages have been earned by the employees, the expense and the related liability must be recorded as of the end of December. The hourly wage rates for each employee are multiplied by the total hours worked resulting in gross pay of $3,000. This amount must be recorded as wages expense in the appropriate departments and as accrued wages. In addition, the spa is also responsible for the employer portion of payroll taxes at 7.65% as of 2004. Assuming none of the 10 employees is over the maximum limit in this regard, another liability and related expense for $229.50 must be recorded ($3,000 × .0765 = $229.50). Other details such as withholding of federal, city, and state taxes should be recorded.

Deferred Revenue—Gift Certificates

Many spas sell gift certificates and immediately receive cash from their clients. These gift certificates will be redeemed by users in the future. Until redeemed, the amount received should be recognized as a liability. As the gift certificates are used, the appropriate revenue is recognized and this liability is accordingly reduced.

Deferred Revenue—Series

Spas sell packages of services that may be used over time—for example, ten massages to be used over the next 12 months. These groups of services are called series. Until redeemed, the amount received in payment for the series should not be recognized as revenue. As the guest returns for each service in the series, the revenue for that service is recognized, deducted from the series, and this liability is reduced.

Deferred Revenue—Other

The unearned portion of membership dues, rentals, etc., are credited to this account if the spa expects to realize the revenue during the 12 months following the balance sheet date. It is strongly recommended that deferred revenue be recorded for membership dues that the spa has received for services that have not yet been provided.

Deferred Rent—Current

This line item includes the unearned portion of rental concessions by landlords as well as differences between amounts paid to landlords and amounts charged to rent expense when leases contain fixed rental increases throughout the lease term. The amount in this caption would include amounts expected to reverse within 12 months of the balance sheet date.

Advance Deposits

This line item includes amounts received to reserve the spa facilities or services that have not been provided as of the balance sheet date. As facilities or services are used in the future, this liability is reduced and the appropriate revenue is recognized.

Deferred Income Taxes, Current

This line item represents the tax effects of temporary differences between the bases of current assets and current liabilities for financial and income tax reporting purposes. For example, revenue recognized in the financial statements before it is taxable will result in current deferred income taxes if it will be taxable in the next year. Current Deferred Income Taxes are presented as net current assets or net current liabilities as circumstances dictate.

Other Current Liabilities

This line item includes current liabilities such as other guest prepaid services not included under line items discussed previously. The nature of these items, if material, should be clearly indicated on the Balance Sheet or in the notes to the financial statements.

Long-Term Debt

This section of the Balance Sheet includes notes and similar liabilities and obligations under capital leases that are not due within 12 months of the balance sheet date. Either the Balance Sheet itself or notes accompanying the financial statements should disclose the following information relative to long-term debt other than obligations under capital leases:

- Interest rates
- Amortization or sinking fund requirements
- Maturity dates
- Debt collateralized and assets pledged
- Financial restrictive covenants
- Required principal and sinking fund payments for each year in the five-year period subsequent to the balance sheet date

Disclosure requirements for obligations under capital leases include total future minimum lease payments as of the balance sheet date and for each year in the five-year period after the balance sheet date, recorded at net present value. Amounts lent to the company by owners and officers should be disclosed here.

Deferred Revenue—Noncurrent

The unearned portion of membership dues and other revenue items are charged to this account if the spa expects to realize the revenue in periods beyond 12 months from the balance sheet date.

Deferred Rent—Noncurrent

This account includes the portion of deferred rent that is not expected to reverse within 12 months of the balance sheet date.

Deferred Income Taxes—Noncurrent

This line item includes amounts that represent the tax effects of timing differences attributable to the differences in the bases or carrying amounts of the assets and liabilities between financial statement reporting and income tax reporting. Such carrying amount differences arise from items such as different useful lives for depreciating property and equipment. The calculation of deferred income tax liabilities is a complex process and management should seek the advice of their accountants for additional guidance.

Deferred income tax assets and liabilities are generally material only for C corporations that pay substantial income taxes. Partnerships, sole proprietorships, and S corporations are generally not affected by deferred income taxes.

Other Long-Term Liabilities

This section of the Balance Sheet includes long-term liabilities that cannot be listed under accounts discussed previously, such as with the provision of long-term leases that are not payable or refundable within 12 months of the balance sheet date. Other examples include deferred compensation, deferred management fees, and refundable membership deposits. The nature of these items, if material, should be clearly indicated on the Balance Sheet or in the Notes to the Financial Statements.

OWNERS' EQUITY

The Owners' Equity section of the Balance Sheet is presented differently for corporations, partnerships, limited liability companies, and sole proprietorships, depending upon the type of equity ownership. Presentation formats are shown on page 6. Examples of detailed presentations of Statements of Owners' Equity are shown in Section 3.

Corporation

Stockholders' Equity

Capital Stock. Capital stock denotes the shares of ownership of a corporation that have been authorized by its articles of incorporation. The most prevalent classes of capital stock are preferred and common stock. The par or stated value and the number of shares authorized and issued for each class of stock should be presented in the Balance Sheet. Changes during the period should be shown in the Statement of Shareholders' Equity.

Additional Paid-In Capital. Additional paid-in capital includes cash, property, and other capital contributed to a corporation by its stockholders in excess of the stated or par value of capital stock. Changes during the period should be shown in the Statement of Stockholders' Equity.

Other Comprehensive Income. As of the balance sheet date, the total of other comprehensive income must be shown separately from retained earnings and additional paid-in capital. Comprehensive income includes charges or credits to equity that are not the result of transactions with owners (e.g., cumulative foreign currency translation adjustments, minimum pension liabilities, unrealized gains and losses on available-for-sale securities, the effective portion of the change in the fair value of cash flow and net investment hedges, etc.). The determination of items of comprehensive income is often complex and management should consult with accountants to ensure appropriate items are identified. Changes during the period should be shown in the Statement of Stockholders' Equity.

Retained Earnings. Retained earnings represent the accumulated net income not distributed as dividends but retained in the business. Changes during the period should be shown in the Statement of Stockholders' Equity. Negative Retained Earnings are generally referred to as accumulated deficits.

Treasury Stock. Treasury stock represents the cost of the company's stock acquired by the company and not retired and should be reflected as a reduction in total Stockholders' Equity. Changes during the period should be shown in the Statement of Stockholders' Equity.

Partnership

Partners' Equity

Partners' equity represents the net equity of the partners in the partnership and should be classified where appropriate as general and limited partners' equity. Changes during the period should be shown in the Statement of Partners' Equity.

Other Comprehensive Income. As of the balance sheet date, the total of other comprehensive income must be shown separately from retained earnings and additional paid-in capital. Comprehensive income includes charges or credits to equity that are not the result of transactions with owners (e.g., cumulative foreign currency translation adjustments, minimum pension liabilities, unrealized gains and losses on available-for-sale securities, the effective portion of the change in the fair value of cash flow and net investment hedges, etc.). The determination of items of comprehensive income is often complex and management should consult with accountants to ensure appropriate items are identified. Changes during the period should be shown in the Statement of Partners' Equity.

Contributions. Contributions include the amount of any additional assets that are invested in the business by the partners during the period just ended.

Withdrawals. Withdrawals include the amount of any assets that are taken out of the business and distributed to the partners during the period just ended.

Limited Liability Company

Members' Equity

Members' equity represents the net equity of the members in the limited liability company. Changes during the period should be shown in the Statement of Members' Equity.

Other Comprehensive Income. As of the balance sheet date, the total of other comprehensive income must be shown separately from retained earnings and additional paid-in capital. Comprehensive income includes charges or credits to equity that are not the result of transactions with owners (e.g., cumulative foreign currency translation adjustments, minimum pension liabilities, unrealized gains and losses on available-for-sale securities, the effective portion of the change in the fair value of cash flow and net investment hedges, etc.). The determination of items of comprehensive income is often complex and management should consult with accountants to ensure appropriate items are identified. Changes during the period should be shown in the Statement of Members' Equity.

Contributions. Contributions include the amount of any additional assets that are invested in the business by the members during the period just ended.

Withdrawals. Withdrawals include the amount of any assets that are taken out of the business and distributed to the members during the period just ended.

Sole Proprietorship

Owner's Equity

The Owner's Equity of a sole proprietorship is similar to the equity of a partnership except that it represents the interest of one individual as opposed to a number of partners. Changes during the period should be shown in the Statement of Owners' Equity.

Other Comprehensive Income. As of the balance sheet date, the total of other comprehensive income must be shown separately from retained earnings and additional paid-in capital. Comprehensive income includes charges or credits to equity that are not the result of transactions with owners (e.g., cumulative foreign currency translation adjustments, minimum pension liabilities, unrealized gains and losses on available-for-sale securities, the effective portion of the change in the fair value of cash flow and net investment hedges, etc.). The determination of items of comprehensive income is often complex and management should consult with accountants to ensure appropriate items are identified. Changes during the period should be shown in the Statement of Owner's Equity.

Contributions. Contributions include the amount of any additional assets that are invested in the business by the owner during the period just ended.

Withdrawals. Withdrawals include the amount of any assets that are taken out of the business and distributed to the owner during the period just ended.

Format of Accounts Outside the United States

The examples and formats used throughout this book follow U.S. accounting standards for the presentation of financial statements. Users of the book outside the United States should be aware that the accounting requirements of their own jurisdictions will not necessarily follow those of the United States. The laws of other jurisdictions and the application of accounting standards may significantly affect the format and presentation of financial statements.

For example, countries that are Member States of the European Union must follow the layout prescribed for company accounts in the European Fourth Directive on Company Accounts—a layout that is quite different from the U.S. standard. Other jurisdictions have no legal requirements and so whatever layout is considered most appropriate in those circumstances may be used.

Section 2
Statement of Income

The Statement of Income reflects the results of operations for a period of time. The time covered by this statement usually ends at the balance sheet date. When the statement reflects a net loss, the title is generally changed to Statement of Operations.

Spa organizations prepare income statements for both external users (e.g., potential investors, creditors, and owners not active in managing the business) and internal users (i.e., managers of the business). These statements differ in the amount of information presented. The statement presented to external users is relatively brief, providing only summary detail about the results of operations.

Two sample formats for external users are shown here. The degree of detail presented in the statements is somewhat discretionary although the following captions—revenue, expenses, interest, depreciation, and income taxes—should be presented unless the amounts are insignificant. To the extent that any individual revenue or expense item is significant, separate disclosure should be made. A format useful for managers operating the spa is discussed in Section 6.

STATEMENT OF INCOME

	Period	
	Current Year	**Prior Year**
NET REVENUE	$	$
TOTAL DIRECT EXPENSES		
GROSS MARGIN		
TOTAL INDIRECT AND UNDISTRIBUTED EXPENSES		
INCOME BEFORE FIXED CHARGES		
FIXED CHARGES		
INCOME BEFORE DEPRECIATION AND AMORTIZATION, INTEREST EXPENSE AND INCOME TAXES		
Depreciation		
Amortization		
Interest		
(Gain) and Loss on Disposal of Property		
INCOME BEFORE INCOME TAXES		
INCOME TAXES		
NET INCOME	$	$

STATEMENT OF INCOME

	Period	
	Current Year	Prior Year
NET REVENUE		
Massage	$	$
Skin Care		
Hair		
Nail		
Fitness		
Food and Beverage		
Health and Wellness		
Memberships		
Retail		
Rentals and Other		
Other Operating Activities		
Total Net Revenue		
COST OF GOODS AND DIRECT EXPENSES		
Massage		
Skin Care		
Hair		
Nail		
Fitness		
Food and Beverage		
Health and Wellness		
Retail		
Other Operating Activities		
Total Direct Expenses		
GROSS MARGIN		
INDIRECT EXPENSES		
Indirect Operating Expenses		
Indirect Support Labor		
Total Indirect Expenses		
UNDISTRIBUTED OPERATING EXPENSES		
General and Administrative		
Marketing		
Facility Maintenance and Utilities		
Total Undistributed Operating Expenses		
INCOME BEFORE FIXED CHARGES		
FIXED CHARGES		
Insurance		
Management Fees		
Rent		
Real Estate/Personal Property Taxes		
Total Fixed Charges		
INCOME BEFORE DEPRECIATION AND AMORTIZATION, INTEREST EXPENSE AND INCOME TAXES		
Depreciation		
Amortization		
Interest Expense		
(Gain) and Loss on Disposal of Property		
INCOME BEFORE INCOME TAXES		
INCOME TAXES		
NET INCOME	$	$

Section 3
Statement of Owners' Equity

A separate Statement of Owners' Equity should be presented if there is significant activity in the accounts during the period. If net income or loss is the only change to the equity accounts in the period, it is permissible to reconcile the change in retained earnings at the bottom of the Statement of Income and exclude presentation of the separate owners' equity statement. The format of the owners' equity statement will depend on the type of entity. The following pages show examples of the types of presentation for corporations, partnerships, and sole proprietorships.

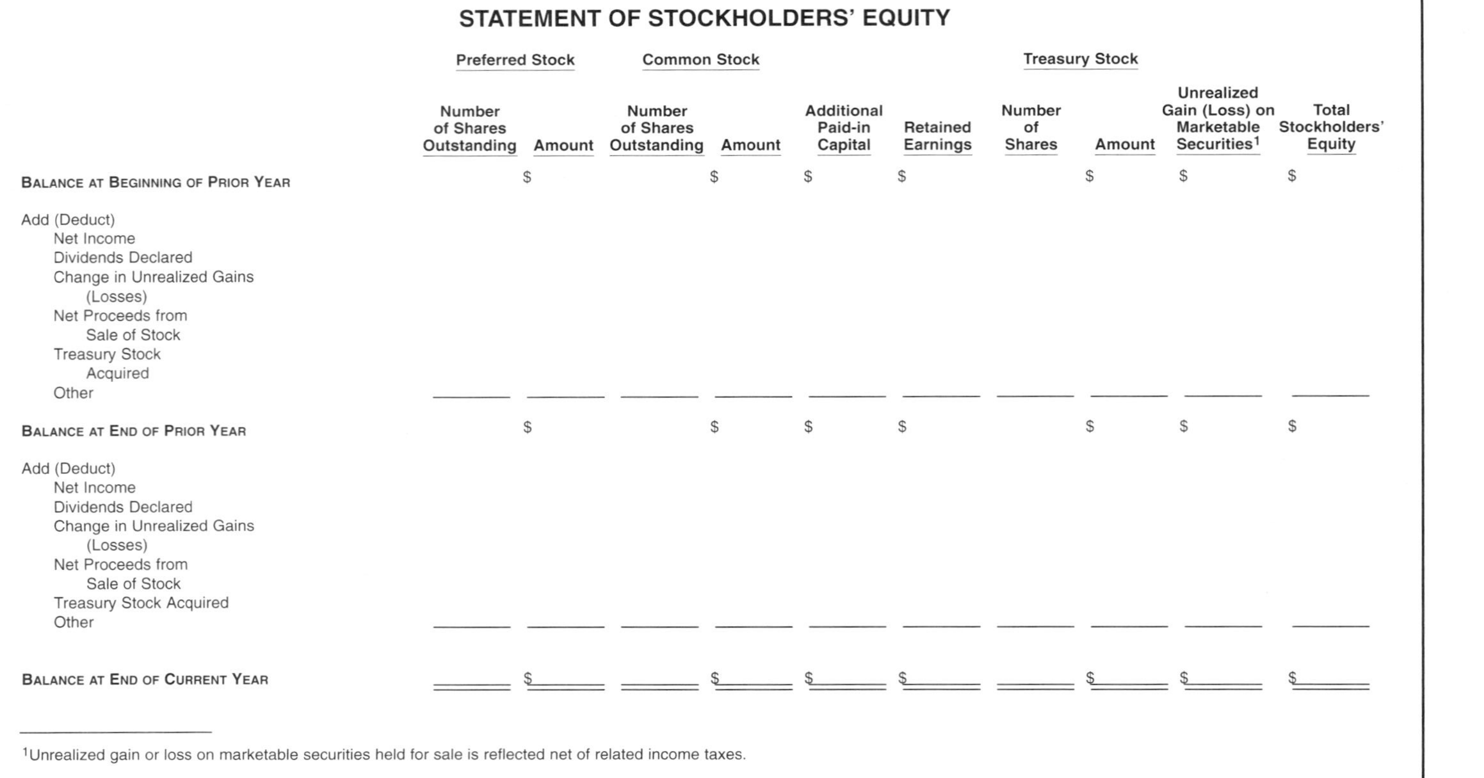

STATEMENT OF STOCKHOLDERS' EQUITY

	Preferred Stock		Common Stock				Treasury Stock			
	Number of Shares Outstanding	Amount	Number of Shares Outstanding	Amount	Additional Paid-in Capital	Retained Earnings	Number of Shares	Amount	Unrealized Gain (Loss) on Marketable Securities[1]	Total Stockholders' Equity
BALANCE AT BEGINNING OF PRIOR YEAR		$		$	$	$		$	$	$
Add (Deduct)										
Net Income										
Dividends Declared										
Change in Unrealized Gains (Losses)										
Net Proceeds from Sale of Stock										
Treasury Stock Acquired										
Other										
BALANCE AT END OF PRIOR YEAR		$		$	$	$		$	$	$
Add (Deduct)										
Net Income										
Dividends Declared										
Change in Unrealized Gains (Losses)										
Net Proceeds from Sale of Stock										
Treasury Stock Acquired										
Other										
BALANCE AT END OF CURRENT YEAR		$		$	$	$		$	$	$

[1]Unrealized gain or loss on marketable securities held for sale is reflected net of related income taxes.

STATEMENT OF PARTNERS' EQUITY

	General Partners	Limited Partners	Unrealized Gain (Loss) on Marketable Securities[1]	Total
Balance at Beginning of Prior Year	$	$	$	$
Add (Deduct)				
Net Income				
Contributions				
Change in Unrealized Gains (Losses)				
Withdrawals				
Other				
Balance at End of Prior Year	$	$	$	$
Add (Deduct)				
Net Income				
Contributions				
Change in Unrealized Gains (Losses)				
Withdrawals				
Other				
Balance at End of Current Year	$	$	$	$

[1]Unrealized gain or loss on marketable securities held for sale is reflected net of related income taxes.

STATEMENT OF OWNER'S EQUITY

	Owner	Unrealized Gain (Loss) on Marketable Securities[1]	Total
Balance at Beginning of Prior Year	$	$	$
Add (Deduct)			
Net Income			
Contributions			
Change in Unrealized Gains (Losses)			
Withdrawals			
Other			
Balance at End of Prior Year	$	$	$
Add (Deduct)			
Net Income			
Contributions			
Change in Unrealized Gains (Losses)			
Withdrawals			
Other			
Balance at End of Current Year	$	$	$

[1]Unrealized gain or loss on marketable securities held for sale is reflected net of related income taxes.

Section 4
Statement of Cash Flows

The Statement of Cash Flows summarizes the change in Cash and Equivalents over the same period of time as that covered by the Statement of Income. Cash equivalents are readily convertible investments, such as treasury bills, certificates of deposit, and commercial paper, with original maturities of less than three months. The change in Cash and Equivalents is classified as coming from three activities: operating, investing, and financing.

Cash flows from operating activities represent the amount of cash generated by spa operations. Operating activities include transactions involving acquiring, selling, and delivering goods for sale, as well as providing services. Cash flows from operating activities for a spa include cash receipts collected from guests, cash disbursments paid to employees and other suppliers, interest paid and received, taxes paid, and other operating payments and receipts. The operating activities section of the Statement of Cash Flows measures the amount that net income would have been if the cash method were used for measuring revenues and expenses.

Cash flows from investing activities represent changes in cash arising from transactions related to asset accounts that do not affect operations. Transactions include acquisition and disposal of property and equipment as well as the purchase and sale of investments, whether they are current or noncurrent.

Cash flows from financing activities represent cash changes related to liability and equity accounts that do not affect operations. These include obtaining and repaying debt (whether current or noncurrent), issuing and repurchasing stock, and dividend payments.

Cash flows from operating activities can be computed using either the direct or indirect approach. The direct method identifies the operating cash receipts and cash disbursements. The indirect method determines the cash from operations by adjusting net income for noncash items. The indirect method is useful for identifying why net income differs from cash from operating activities. Because the indirect method is overwhelmingly used in all industries, it is the only approach shown in this book.

While the Statement of Cash Flows summarizes all significant sources and uses of cash, there is also a requirement to disclose significant noncash investing and financing activities. This information is generally presented in narrative form immediately below the Statement. Items that should be disclosed include the purchase of capital assets by incurring debt or through capital lease transactions. Transactions involving the sale of assets where the seller provides financing is another example requiring disclosure. Lastly, the amount of cash paid for interest and income taxes is also required to be disclosed.

Statement of Cash Flows

	Period	
	Current Year	**Prior Year**
CASH FLOWS FROM OPERATING ACTIVITIES		
Net Income	$	$
Adjustments to Reconcile Net Income to Cash Provided by (Used in) Operating Activities:		
Add: Depreciation and Amortization		
Gain (Loss) on Sale of Property and Equipment		
Deferred Taxes		
(Increase) Decrease in:		
Short-Term Investments		
Receivables, Net		
Inventories		
Prepaid Expenses		
Other Current Assets		
Increase (Decrease) in:		
Accounts Payable		
Income Taxes Payable		
Accrued Expenses		
Deferred Revenues		
Advance Desposits		
Other Current Liabilities		
Net Cash Provided by (Used in) Operating Activities		
CASH FLOWS FROM INVESTING ACTIVITIES		
Capital Expenditures		
Proceeds from Asset Dispositions		
Proceeds from Sale of Investments		
Purchases of Investments		
Net Cash Provided by (Used in) Investing Activities		
CASH FLOWS FROM FINANCING ACTIVITIES		
Proceeds from Debt Financing		
Debt Repayments		
Proceeds from Equity Financing		
Distribution to Owners		
Net Cash Provided by (Used in) Financing Activities		
INCREASE (DECREASE) IN CASH AND EQUIVALENTS		
CASH AND EQUIVALENTS, BEGINNING OF PERIOD		
CASH AND EQUIVALENTS, END OF PERIOD	$	$
CASH PAID FOR INTEREST	$	$
CASH PAID FOR INCOME TAXES	$	$

SUPPLEMENTAL INFORMATION RELATED TO NONCASH INVESTING AND FINANCING ACTIVITIES (DISCLOSE SIGNIFICANT ITEMS SEPARATELY.)

Cash Flows from Operating Activities

Net Income and Depreciation and Amortization

These amounts are obtained directly from the Income Statement.

Gain (Loss) on Sale of Property and Equipment

This is the gain or loss included in the determination of net income.

Deferred Taxes

This is the net change of all deferred tax accounts (current and noncurrent) included on the Balance Sheet.

Changes in Current Assets and Current Liabilities

These lines reflect the net change in the comparable balance sheet accounts for the periods presented.

Cash Flows from Investing Activities

Capital Expenditures

Capital expenditures represent payments to purchase property, buildings, equipment, and other productive assets. These payments include interest payments capitalized as part of the cost of those assets. Separating cash payments that represent an increase in revenue-generating capacity from cash payments that are required to maintain operating capacity is helpful in enabling users to determine whether the spa is investing adequately in the maintenance of its operating capacity.

Proceeds from Asset Dispositions

This line item includes the proceeds from asset dispositions, reduced by selling cost payments. This item should not include any amount of the sales consideration that has been financed by the seller. Such disclosure would be included supplementally in narrative form.

Proceeds from Sale of Investments

This line item includes the net proceeds from the sale of investments, after deduction of selling expenses.

Purchases of Investments

This line item includes the purchase price paid for investments, including the transaction costs paid.

Cash Flows from Financing Activities

Proceeds from Debt Financing

This line item includes the net proceeds after deduction of transaction costs. This item includes both long- and short-term financing.

Debt Repayments

This line item includes aggregate principal repayments on indebtedness.

Proceeds from Equity Financing

This line item includes the net proceeds after deduction of transaction costs.

Distributions to Owners

This line item includes the amount of dividends paid to owners. Other distributions to owners should be included, with appropriate modification of the caption, if the entity is not a corporation.

Section 5
Notes to the Financial Statements

In order for a financial presentation to be complete, explanatory notes should accompany the financial statements. The notes should describe all significant accounting policies followed by the spa. Commonly required disclosures include, but are not limited to, policies regarding the following:

- Basis of consolidation
- Use of estimates
- Cash and temporary cash investments
- Inventory methods and valuation
- Accounting for investments, including the valuation of marketable securities
- Depreciation and amortization policies
- Accounting for deferred charges
- Advertising costs
- Accounting for pensions
- Revenue recognition
- Accounting for income taxes
- Computation of net income (loss) per share (public companies only)
- Fair value of financial instruments
- Concentrations of credit risk

Disclosure of accounting policy-related footnotes should be followed by such additional notes as are necessary to provide for full disclosure of all significant events or conditions reflected in the financial statements, or as otherwise required by the rules of professional accounting or regulatory organizations. Typical events and conditions that are disclosed in the notes accompanying financial statements include the following:

- Changes in accounting methods
- Long-term debt agreements
- Pension and/or profit-sharing plans
- Other post-retirement and post-employment benefits
- Income taxes
- Long-term contracts

- Stock option plans
- Extraordinary items of income or expense
- Significant long-term commitments, including leases
- Foreign operations
- Related party transactions
- Contingent liabilities, including pending litigation
- Stockholders' equity transactions
- Financial instruments
- Impairment or disposal of long-lived assets
- Restructuring costs
- Extinguishment of debt
- Discontinued operations
- Business combinations
- Accumulated other comprehensive income (loss)
- Business segment information (public companies only)
- Quarterly financial information (public companies only)
- Organization (geographic and nature of business)
- Concentration of credit risk
- Subsequent events

Section 6
Departmental Statements

The Departmental Statements of Income reflect the results of operations for a given period. They provide some of the most important internal sources of information for spa managers.

It is suggested that an overall Summary Statement of Income be prepared with supporting schedules of revenues and expenses for each of the departments or activities in the property. The Summary Statement of Income, shown on page 33, is divided into several sections. The Spa Departments section of the Summary Statement of Income reports the Net Revenue, Cost of Sales, Payroll and Related Expenses, Other Expenses, and Income (Loss) for the four spa revenue-producing departments of the property.

Indirect Expenses related to the spa departments, including support labor and operating expenses, are subtracted to determine Spa After Indirect Expenses.

Memberships and Other Operated Departments are reported next. Details for these departments include the Net Revenue, Cost of Sales, Payroll and Related Expenses, Other Expenses, and Income (Loss). The totals for memberships and other departments are added to Spa After Indirect Expenses to obtain Income Before Undistributed Expenses.

The Undistributed Operating Expenses section of the Summary Statement of Income reports expenses that are considered applicable to the entire property and are not easily allocated to operated departments.

Income Before Fixed Charges is calculated by subtracting Total Undistributed Operating Expenses from the Income Before Undistributed Expenses.

Fixed Charges, including management fees and rent, property taxes, and insurance, are subtracted from Income Before Fixed Charges to arrive at Income Before Depreciation, Amortization, Interest, and Income Taxes. Depreciation and Amortization and Interest Expenses are then subtracted from the previously calculated amount as the first step to determine Income Before Income Taxes.

On the Summary Statement of Income, Gains on Sale of Property are reported separately from revenues, and Losses on Sale of Property are reported separately from expenses, because these distinctions are important in evaluating the effectiveness of management. Management is primarily held responsible for revenues and expenses associated with operations, and only secondarily (if at all) for gains and losses on the sale of property. Gains are added and losses are subtracted to determine Income Before Income Taxes. Finally, Income Taxes are subtracted to determine Net Income.

The number and types of operated departments and undistributed operating expenses will vary according to the needs and requirements of individual properties. The Summary Statement of Income shown on page 33 presents an extensive list of operated departments for a full-service spa with a wide range of offerings. Therefore, the line items listed on the Summary Statement of Income presented here may not apply to most small spas. Individual spas should modify the Summary Statement of Income to meet their own needs and requirements.

Sample supporting schedules and explanations of line items appearing on them are presented in the pages that follow. The supporting schedule numbers are for cross-reference purposes only.

A sample summary income statement and its supporting schedules are presented in Part III. The suggested statements are presented for guidance only, because it is recognized that it would be impractical to prescribe a single model for every possible situation. The accounting presentation and disclosure in each set of financial statements should include the information necessary in the particular circumstances.

SUMMARY STATEMENT OF INCOME

	Schedule	Net Revenues	Cost of Sales	Payroll and Related Expenses	Other Expenses	Income (Loss)
Spa Departments						
Massage	1	$	$	$	$	$
Skin Care	2					
Nail	3					
Hair	4					
Total Spa Contributions						
Indirect Expenses						
Indirect Support Labor	12					
Indirect Operating Expenses	13					
Total Indirect Expenses						
Spa After Indirect Expenses						
Memberships	8					
Other Operated Departments						
Fitness	5					
Food and Beverage	6					
Health and Wellness	7					
Retail	9					
Other Operating Departments	10					
Rentals and Other Income	11					
Total Other Operated Departmental Income (Loss)						
Income Before Undistributed Expenses						
Undistributed Operating Expenses						
Administrative and General	14					
Marketing	15					
Facilities Maintenance and Utilities	16					
Total Undistributed Operating Expenses						
Totals		$	$	$	$	
Income Before Fixed Charges						
Fixed Charges	17					
Income Before Depreciation, Amortization, Interest and Income Taxes						
Depreciation and Amortization	17					
Interest Expense	17					
Gain or Loss on Disposal of Property	17					
Income Before Income Taxes						
Income Taxes	18					
Net Income						$

Massage—Schedule 1

	Current Period
REVENUE	
Massage	
Relaxation and Therapeutic	$
Specialty	
Total Massage	
Body Treatments	
Hydrotherapy	
Wraps and Scrubs	
Specialty Body Treatments	
Total Body Treatments	
Other	
Breakage	
Service Charges	
Other Revenue	
Total Other	
TOTAL REVENUE	
ALLOWANCES	
NET REVENUE	
DIRECT EXPENSES	
Payroll and Related Expenses	
Salaries and Wages	
Commissions	
Contract	
Distributed Service Charges	
Payroll Taxes and Employee Benefits	
Total Payroll and Related Expenses	
Other—Professional Products and Supplies	
TOTAL DIRECT EXPENSES	
DEPARTMENTAL CONTRIBUTION	$

Massage—Schedule 1 illustrates a format and identifies line items that commonly appear on a supplemental schedule supporting amounts appearing on the Summary Statement of Income for Spa Departments—Massage. The format and line items will vary according to the needs and requirements of individual spas, which should modify the schedule to meet their own needs and requirements. Larger spa operations may choose to insert additional revenue categories to further distinguish revenue composition. Smaller spa operations that are unable to collect the information necessary to distribute revenues into the major treatment categories may choose instead to use *Massage—Schedule 1S* (short), shown in Section 7. Direct expenses that can be identified for specific treatments are included on the departmental schedule to determine the contribution of the massage department to the overall spa operation.

Note: In some spas, body treatments are provided by the skin care technicians; in those cases, the body treatment revenues shown on *Massage—Schedule 1* should instead be reflected on *Skin Care—Schedule 2* in order to more easily track Payroll and Related Expenses.

Revenue

Massage

Relaxation and Therapeutic. This account includes revenue derived from various types of massage treatments, including Swedish, sports, deep tissue, neck, and shoulder massage services.

Specialty. This account includes revenue derived from specialty massage services such as aromatherapy massage, hot stone massage, reflexology, shiatsu, Thai, pre-natal, reiki, and other types of signature massage treatments.

Total Massage. Total Massage is the sum of Relaxation and Therapeutic and Specialty.

Body Treatments

Hydrotherapy. This account includes revenue derived from various types of hydrotherapy treatments, including hydrotherapy tub treatments, Vichy showers, therapeutic baths, Scotch showers, hot and cold baths, and other water-based body treatments.

Wraps and Scrubs. This account includes revenue derived from various wraps and scrubs, including mud treatments, body wraps such as algae, herbal, or oil, loofah scrubs, salt glows, and other exfoliation or body nourishing treatments.

Specialty Body Treatments. This account includes revenue from specialty body treatments such as pressotherapy, ionithermie, aromazone, body bronzing, cellulite treatments, and other signature body treatments.

Total Body Treatments. Total Body Treatments is the sum of Hydrotherapy, Wraps and Scrubs, and Specialty Body Treatments.

Other

Breakage. This account should be charged with any excess of spa packages sold over the retail price of the individual massage or bodywork treatments, or unused treatments included as part of a spa package.

Service Charges. This account should be used to record the total gross service charges at either a fixed amount or a percentage of sale, collected from guests for massage services and body treatments. The distribution of the service charge to employees is charged to the payroll account Distributed Service Charges and is reflected under the Payroll and Related Expenses section of this schedule.

Other Revenue. This account includes other non-treatment-related revenue such as income from chair and/or space rental.

Total Other. Total Other is the sum of Breakage, Service Charges, and Other Revenue.

Total Revenue

Total Revenue is the sum of Total Massage, Total Body Treatments, and Total Other.

Allowances

This line item includes rebates, refunds, and overcharges of revenue not known at the time of sale but adjusted at a later date. An important financial management practice is tracking coupons, special offers, and other discount programs. Discounts are not included in allowances as they are applied at the time of the sale. Should discounts be significant, a separate discount account may be added to the departmental schedule, which would require reflecting revenues at gross and reduced to net with a discounts account or a managerial discounts report.

Net Revenue

Net Revenue is calculated by subtracting Allowances from Total Revenue.

Direct Expenses

Salaries and Wages

This account includes regular pay, overtime pay, vacation pay, severance pay, holiday pay, and bonuses for employees of the massage department, including those of working massage supervisors. It does not include the salaries and wages of indirect support labor, which are charged to *Schedule 11—Indirect Support Labor.*

Commissions

This account includes compensation to therapists in the form of a percentage commission on individual treatment revenue.

Contract

This account is charged with the cost associated with outsourcing massage services to independent contractor therapists.

Distributed Service Charges

This account reflects the total amount of service charges paid to employees of the massage department. Service charges collected from guests are charged to the Service Charges revenue account.

Payroll Taxes and Employee Benefits

This account includes payroll taxes, payroll-related insurance expenses, and retirement and other payroll-related expenses applicable to the massage department. In many resort and destination spas, meals are provided to the employees. In these cases, an Employee Meals account should be added if the cost is significant.

Total Payroll and Related Expenses

Total Payroll and Related Expenses is the sum of Salaries and Wages, Commissions, Contract, Distributed Service Charges and Payroll Taxes and Employee Benefits.

Other—Professional Products and Supplies

This account is charged with those professional treatment products that are specifically used in the delivery of massage department treatments, such as massage oils, salts, mud, algae, and other treatment products coded to massage services, plus treatment-specific supplies used by the massage therapists such as herbal wrap sheets, oil/lotion warmers, plastic wraps, aromatherapy oils used in massage or hydrotherapy treatments, or massage hot stones. It is a recommended practice to complete a physical inventory of professional products at the end of each accounting period. Any adjustments from book value to actual count are recorded in this account. If the required adjustment is significant, it should be shown on a separate line titled Inventory Adjustment.

Total Direct Expenses

Total Direct Expenses is the sum of Total Payroll and Related Expenses and Other—Professional Products and Supplies.

Departmental Contribution

Departmental Contribution is calculated by subtracting Total Direct Expenses from Net Revenue. The Departmental Contribution is the amount that appears on the Summary Statement of Income in the Income (Loss) column for Spa Departments—Massage.

Skin Care—Schedule 2

	Current Period
REVENUE	
Facial Treatments	
Standard Facials	$
Specialty Facials	______
Total Facial Treatments	______
Waxing Services	
Body Hair Removal	
Face Hair Removal	______
Total Waxing Services	______
Other	
Breakage	
Service Charges	
Other Revenue	______
Total Other	______
TOTAL REVENUE	
ALLOWANCES	______
NET REVENUE	
DIRECT EXPENSES	
Payroll and Related Expenses	
Salaries and Wages	
Commissions	
Contract	
Distributed Service Charges	
Payroll Taxes and Employee Benefits	______
Total Payroll and Related Expenses	______
Other—Professional Products and Supplies	______
TOTAL DIRECT EXPENSES	______
DEPARTMENTAL CONTRIBUTION	$______

Skin Care—Schedule 2 illustrates a format and identifies line items that commonly appear on a supplemental schedule supporting amounts appearing on the Summary Statement of Income for Spa Departments—Skin Care. The format and line items will vary according to the needs and requirements of individual spas, which should modify the schedule to meet their own needs and requirements. Larger spa operations may choose to insert additional revenue categories to further distinguish revenue composition. Smaller spa operations that are unable to collect the information necessary to distribute revenues into the major treatment categories may choose instead to use *Skin Care—Schedule 2S* (short), shown in Section 7. Direct expenses that can be identified for specific treatments are included on the departmental schedule to determine the contribution of the skin care department to the overall spa operation.

Note: In some spas, body treatments are provided by the skin care technicians; in those cases, the body treatment revenue shown on *Massage—Schedule 1* should instead be reflected on *Skin Care—Schedule 2* in order to more easily track Payroll and Related Expenses.

Revenue

Facial Treatments

Standard Facials. This account includes revenue derived from facial treatments, including deep cleansing facials, gentlemen's facials, and mini-facials as examples.

Specialty Facials. This account includes revenue derived from specialty facial services such as collagen facials, anti-aging, oxygen, ampoules, seaweed or layer mask facials, cellular rejuvenation or glycolic facials, or other signature facial treatments.

Total Facial Treatments. Total Facial Treatments is the sum of Standard Facials and Specialty Facials.

Waxing Services

Body Hair Removal. This account includes revenue derived from body hair removal services such as back waxing, sugaring, leg or arm and bikini waxing, and other specialty services such as laser removal.

Face Hair Removal. This account includes revenues from brow waxing, threading, sugaring, lip waxing, and other face waxing procedures.

Total Waxing Services. Total Waxing Services is the sum of Body Hair Removal and Face Hair Removal.

Other

Breakage. This account should be charged with any excess of spa packages sold over the retail price of the individual skin care treatments, or unused Skin Care treatments included as part of a spa package.

Service Charges. This account should be used to record the total gross service charges at either a fixed amount or a percentage of sale, collected from guests for skin care services. The distribution of the service charge to employees is charged to the payroll account Distributed Service Charges and is reflected under the Payroll and Related Expenses section of this schedule.

Other Revenue. This account includes other non-treatment-related revenue such as income from chair and/or space rental.

Total Other. Total Other is the sum of Breakage, Service Charges, and Other Revenue.

Total Revenue

Total Revenue is the sum of Total Facial Treatments, Total Waxing Treatments, and Total Other.

Allowances

This line item includes rebates, refunds, and overcharges of revenue not known at the time of sale but adjusted at a later date. An important financial management practice is tracking coupons, special offers, and other discount programs. Discounts are not included in Allowances as they are applied at the time of the sale. Should discounts be significant, a separate discount account may be added to the departmental schedule, which would require reflecting revenues at gross and reduced to net with a discounts account or a managerial discounts report.

Net Revenue

Net revenue is calculated by subtracting Allowances from Total revenue.

Direct Expenses

Salaries and Wages

This account includes regular pay, overtime pay, vacation pay, severance pay, holiday pay, and bonuses for employees of the skin care department, including those of working skin care supervisors. It does not include the salaries and wages of indirect support labor, which are charged to *Schedule 11—Indirect Support Labor.*

Commissions

This account includes compensation to skin care technicians (aestheticians) in the form of a percentage commission on individual treatment revenue.

Contract

This account is charged with the cost associated with outsourcing skin care services to independent contractor technicians.

Distributed Service Charges

This account reflects the total amount of service charges paid to employees of the skin care department. Service charges collected from guests are charged to the Service Charge revenue account.

Payroll Taxes and Employee Benefits

This account includes payroll taxes, payroll-related insurance expenses, and retirement and other payroll-related expenses applicable to the skin care department. In many resort and destination spas, meals are provided to the employee. In these cases, an Employee Meals account should be added if the cost is significant.

Total Payroll and Related Expenses

Total Payroll and Related Expenses is the sum of Salaries and Wages, Commissions, Contract, Distributed Service Charges, and Payroll Taxes and Employee Benefits.

Other—Professional Products and Supplies

This account is charged with those professional treatment products that are specifically used in the delivery of skin care department treatments, such as cleansers and masques, plus treatment-specific supplies used by the skin care technicians such as paraffin wax, brushes and utensils, waxing strips, and eye pads. It is a recommended practice to complete a physical inventory of professional products at the end of each accounting period. Any adjustments from book value to actual count are recorded in this account. If the required adjustment is significant, it should be shown on a separate line titled Inventory Adjustment.

Total Direct Expenses

Total Direct Expenses is the sum of the Total Payroll and Related Expenses and Other—Professional Products and Supplies.

Departmental Contribution

Departmental Contribution is calculated by subtracting Total Direct Expenses from Net Revenue. The Departmental Contribution is the amount that appears on the Summary Statement of Income in the Income (Loss) column for Spa Departments—Skin Care.

Hair—Schedule 3

	Current Period
REVENUE	
Color and Chemical	
Color	$
Perms and Relaxers	
Total Color and Chemical	
Styling	
Extensions	
Haircuts	
Specialty Styling	
Total Styling	
Other	
Breakage	
Service Charges	
Other Revenue	
Total Other	
TOTAL REVENUE	
ALLOWANCES	
NET REVENUE	
DIRECT EXPENSES	
Payroll and Related Expenses	
Salaries and Wages	
Commissions	
Contract	
Distributed Service Charges	
Payroll Taxes and Employee Benefits	
Total Payroll and Related Expenses	
Other—Professional Products and Supplies	
TOTAL DIRECT EXPENSES	
DEPARTMENTAL CONTRIBUTION	$

Hair—Schedule 3 illustrates a format and identifies line items that commonly appear on a supplemental schedule supporting amounts appearing on the Summary Statement of Income for Spa Departments—Hair. The format and line items will vary according to the needs and requirements of individual spas, which should modify the schedule to meet their own needs and requirements. Larger spa operations may choose to insert additional revenue categories to further distinguish revenue composition. Smaller spa operations that are unable to collect the information necessary to distribute revenues into the major treatment categories may choose instead to use *Hair—Schedule 3S* (short), shown in Section 7. Direct expenses that can be identified for specific treatments are included on the departmental schedule to determine the contribution of the hair services department to the overall spa operation.

Revenue

Color and Chemical

Color. This account includes revenue derived from various types of color hair services, including single process, double process, retouch, glossing, and highlights full or partial.

Perms and Relaxers. This account includes revenue derived from chemical hair services, including partial/full permanents, spirals, full relaxers, and straightening.

Total Color and Chemical. Total Color and Chemical is the sum of Color and Perms and Relaxers.

Styling

Extensions. This account includes revenue derived from full or partial extensions.

Haircuts. This account includes revenue derived from short and long haircuts for women, men, and children.

Specialty Styling. This account includes revenue derived from updo, formal, thermal, braiding, hair and scalp treatments, and other specialty styling services.

Total Styling. Total Styling is the sum of Extensions, Haircuts, and Specialty Styling.

Other

Breakage. This account should be charged with any excess of salon packages sold over the retail price of the individual hair treatments, or unused hair treatments included as part of a salon package.

Service Charges. This account should be used to record the total gross service charges at either a fixed amount or a percentage of sale, collected from guests for salon services. The distribution of the service charges to employees is charged to the payroll account Distributed Service Charges and is reflected under the Payroll and Related Expenses section of this schedule.

Other Revenue. This account includes other non-treatment-related revenue such as income from chair and/or space rental.

Total Other. Total Other is the sum of Breakage, Service Charges, and Other Revenue.

Total Revenue

Total Revenue is the sum of Total Color and Chemical, Total Styling, and Total Other.

Allowances

This line item includes rebates, refunds, and overcharges of revenue not known at the time of sale but adjusted at a later date. An important financial management practice is tracking coupons, special offers, and other discount programs. Discounts are not included in Allowances as they are applied at the time of the sale.

Should discounts be significant, a separate discount account may be added to the departmental schedule, which would require reflecting revenues at gross and reduced to net with a discounts account or a managerial discounts report.

Net Revenue

Net revenue is calculated by subtracting Allowances from Total Revenue.

Direct Expenses

Salaries and Wages

This account includes regular pay, overtime pay, vacation pay, severance pay, holiday pay, and bonuses for employees of the hair salon department, including those of working hair salon supervisors. It does not include the salaries and wages of indirect support labor, which are charged to *Schedule 11—Indirect Support Labor.*

Commissions

This account includes compensation to hair stylists in the form of a percentage commission on individual treatment revenue.

Contract

This account is charged with the cost associated with outsourcing hair services to independent contractor stylists.

Distributed Service Charges

This account reflects the total amount of service charges paid to employees of the hair salon department. Service charges collected from guests are charged to the Service Charges revenue account.

Payroll Taxes and Employee Benefits

This account includes payroll taxes, payroll-related insurance expenses, and retirement and other payroll-related expenses applicable to the hair salon department. In many resort and destination spas, meals are provided to the employee. In these cases, an Employee Meals account should be added if the cost is significant.

Total Payroll and Related Expenses

Total Payroll and Related Expenses is the sum of Salaries and Wages, Commissions, Contract, Distributed Service Charges, and Payroll Taxes and Employee Benefits.

Other—Professional Products and Supplies

This account is charged with those professional treatment products that are specifically used in the delivery of hair department treatments, such as shampoo, conditioner, perm solution, bleach, and other treatment products coded to hair services, plus treatment-specific supplies used by the hair stylists such as tin foil and paper sleeves. It is a recommended practice to complete a physical inventory of professional products at the end of each accounting period. Any adjustments from book value to actual count are recorded in this account. If the required adjustment is significant, it should be shown on a separate line titled Inventory Adjustment.

Total Direct Expenses

Total Direct Expenses is the sum of Total Payroll and Related Expenses and Other—Professional Products and Supplies.

Departmental Contribution

Departmental Contribution is calculated by subtracting Total Direct Expenses from Net Revenue. The Departmental Contribution is the amount that appears on the Summary Statement of Income in the Income (Loss) column for Spa Departments—Hair.

Nail—Schedule 4

	Current Period
Revenue	
Manicure	
Nail Enhancements	$
Specialty Manicure	
Standard Manicure	
Total Manicure	
Pedicure	
Specialty Pedicure	
Standard Pedicure	
Total Pedicure	
Other	
Breakage	
Service Charges	
Other Revenue	
Total Other	
Total Revenue	
Allowances	
Net Revenue	
Direct Expenses	
Payroll and Related Expenses	
Salaries and Wages	
Commissions	
Contract	
Distributed Service Charges	
Payroll Taxes and Employee Benefits	
Total Payroll and Related Expenses	
Other—Professional Products and Supplies	
Total Direct Expenses	
Departmental Contribution	$

Nail—Schedule 4 illustrates a format and identifies line items that commonly appear on a supplemental schedule supporting amounts appearing on the Summary Statement of Income for Spa Departments—Nail. The format and line items will vary according to the needs and requirements of individual spas, which should modify the schedule to meet their own needs and requirements. Larger spa operations may choose to insert additional revenue categories to further distinguish revenue composition. Smaller spa operations that are unable to collect the information necessary to distribute revenues into the major treatment categories may choose instead to use *Nail—Schedule 4S* (short), shown in Section 7. Direct expenses that can be identified for specific treatments are included on the departmental schedule to determine the contribution of the nail department to the overall spa operation.

Revenue

Manicure

Nail Enhancements. This account includes revenue derived from manicure services, such as acrylics, gel tips, silk wraps, fill-ins, French nail tips, and nail repair.

Specialty Manicure. This account includes revenue derived from signature or specialty manicure services, including services such as hot oil, paraffin, special exfoliation, AHA treatments, special masks, anti-aging treatments, and custom blending.

Standard Manicure. This account includes revenue from classic manicures for women or men and polish change.

Total Manicure. Total Manicure is the sum of Nail Enhancements, Specialty Manicure, and Standard Manicure.

Pedicure

Specialty Pedicure. This account includes revenue derived from signature or specialty pedicure services, including hot oil, seaweed, exfoliation treatments, AHA, custom blending, paraffin, and specialty masks.

Standard Pedicure. This account includes revenue from classic pedicures for women or men and polish change.

Total Pedicure. Total Pedicure is the sum of Specialty Pedicure and Standard Pedicure.

Other

Breakage. This account should be charged with any excess of salon packages sold over the retail price of the individual nail treatments, or unused nail treatments included as part of a salon package.

Service Charges. This account should be used to record the total gross service charges either as a fixed amount or a percentage of the sale, collected from guests for nail services. The distribution of the service charges to employees is charged to the payroll account Distributed Service Charges and is reflected under the Payroll and Related Expenses section of this schedule.

Other Revenue. This account includes other non-treatment-related revenue such as income from chair and/or space rental.

Total Other. Total Other is the sum of Breakage, Service Charges, and Other Revenue.

Total Revenue

Total Revenue is the sum of Total Manicure, Total Pedicure, and Total Other.

Allowances

This line item includes rebates, refunds, and overcharges of revenue not known at the time of sale but adjusted at a later date. An important financial management practice is tracking coupons, special offers, and other discount programs.

Discounts are not included in Allowances as they are applied at the time of the sale. Should discounts be significant, a separate discount account may be added to the departmental schedule, which would require reflecting revenues at gross and reduced to net with a discounts account or a managerial discounts report.

Net Revenue

Net Revenue is calculated by subtracting Allowances from Total Revenue.

Direct Expenses

Salaries and Wages

This account includes regular pay, overtime pay, vacation pay, severance pay, holiday pay, and bonuses for employees of the nail salon department, including those of working Nail services supervisors. It does not include the salaries and wages of indirect support labor, which are charged to *Schedule 11—Indirect Support Labor.*

Commissions

This account includes compensation to nail technicians in the form of a percentage commission on individual treatment revenue.

Contract

This account should be charged with the cost associated with outsourcing nail services to independent contractor technicians.

Distributed Service Charges

This account reflects the total amount of service charges paid to employees. Service charges collected from guests are charged to the Service Charges revenue account.

Payroll Taxes and Employee Benefits

This account includes payroll taxes, payroll-related insurance expenses, and retirement and other payroll-related expenses applicable to the nail department. In many resort and destination spas, meals are provided to the employee. In these cases, an Employee Meals account should be added if the cost is significant.

Total Payroll and Related Expenses

Total Payroll and Related Expenses is the sum of Salaries and Wages, Commissions, Contract, Distributed Service Charges, and Payroll Taxes and Employee Benefits.

Other—Professional Products and Supplies

This account is charged with those professional treatment products that are specifically used in the delivery of nail department treatments, such as nail polish, polish remover, and other treatment products coded to nail services, plus treatment-specific supplies used by the nail technicians such as cotton balls, nail polish remover, and nail files. It is a recommended practice to complete a physical inventory of professional products at the end of each accounting period. Any adjustments from book value to actual count are recorded in this account. If the required adjustment is significant, it should be shown on a separate line titled Inventory Adjustment.

Total Direct Expenses

Total Direct Expenses is the sum of Total Payroll and Related Expenses and Other—Professional Products and Supplies.

Departmental Contribution

Departmental Contribution is calculated by subtracting Total Direct Expenses from Net Revenue. The Departmental Contribution is the amount that appears on the Summary Statement of Income in the Income (Loss) column for Spa Departments—Nail.

Fitness—Schedule 5

	Current Period
Revenue	
Personal Training	$
Group Exercise	
Fitness Evaluations	
Service Charges	
Other Revenue	
Total Revenue	
Allowances	
Net Revenue	
Direct Expenses	
Payroll and Related Expenses	
Salaries and Wages	
Commissions	
Contract	
Distributed Service Charges	
Payroll Taxes and Employee Benefits	
Total Payroll and Related Expenses	
Other Expenses	
Ambience	
Athletic Equipment and Supplies	
Contract Services	
Dues and Subscriptions	
Equipment Rental	
Guest Supplies	
Hospitality	
Laundry	
Licenses and Fees	
Linen	
Operating Supplies	
Professional Development	
Telecommunications	
Uniforms	
Other	
Total Other Expenses	
Total Direct Expenses	
Departmental Income (Loss)	$

Fitness—Schedule 5 illustrates a format and identifies line items that commonly appear on a supplemental schedule supporting the amounts reported on the Summary Statement of Income for Other Operated Departments—Fitness. This format and the line items will vary according to the needs and requirements of individual spas, which should modify the schedule to meet their own needs and requirements. If in relation to the total revenue or expense of the fitness department, an item or group of similar items generates significant revenue or expense, the item or group may be listed separately under the appropriate revenue or expense item as a subcategory. For example, some spas may wish to add more detail as subcategories of Group Exercise to identify revenues from aerobics, yoga, or spinning classes. Other spas may have extensive aquatics or hiking programs or racquetball or tennis court fees. These should be recorded as additional revenue categories rather than be shown under Other Revenue.

Many spa fitness departments charge a daily use fee, but may not have a membership program. For those spas that have a membership program including initiation fee and/or monthly dues, the daily use fee revenues appear on *Membership—Schedule 8*. For those spas with no membership program, a daily use fee revenue line should be added to the fitness schedule if the revenue is significant.

Revenue

Personal Training

This accounts includes revenue derived from using qualified fitness professionals to teach personal training to guests and members in private or semi-private sessions.

Group Exercise

This account includes revenue derived from fitness classes such as aerobics, spinning, step classes, and kickboxing conducted in a group format.

Fitness Evaluations

This account includes revenue derived from fitness testing to evaluate a guest's or member's level of health and fitness.

Service Charges

This account should be used to record the total gross service charges collected from guests for fitness services that have an automatic service charge applied to the cost of the service either as a fixed amount or as a percentage of the service. The distribution of the service charge to employees is charged to the payroll account Distributed Service Charges and is reflected under the Payroll and Related Expenses section of this schedule.

Other Revenue

This account includes revenue from the fitness department not identified in the revenue classifications listed. Examples might include revenue from swimming lessons, walking or running programs, and dance or martial arts lessons. If the revenue from any program is significant, the spa should show the revenue on a separate line in this schedule.

Total Revenue

Total Revenue is the sum of Personal Training, Group Exercise, Fitness Evaluations, Service Charges, and Other Revenue.

Allowances

This account includes rebates, refunds, and overcharges of revenue not known at the time of sale but adjusted at a later date.

Net Revenue

Net Revenue is calculated by subtracting Allowances from Total Revenue.

Direct Expenses

Salaries and Wages

This account includes regular pay, overtime pay, vacation pay, severance pay, holiday pay, and bonuses for employees of the fitness department, including those of salaried managers and working fitness supervisors.

Commissions

This account includes compensation to fitness employees in the form of a percentage commission on individual services provided.

Contract

This account should be charged with the cost associated with outsourcing fitness classes or services to independent contractor instructors.

Distributed Service Charges

This account reflects the total amount of service charges paid to fitness employees. Service charges collected from guests are charged to the Service Charges revenue account.

Payroll Taxes and Employee Benefits

This account includes payroll taxes, payroll-related insurance expenses, and retirement and other payroll-related expenses applicable to the fitness department. In many resort and destination spas, meals are provided to the employees. In these cases, an Employee Meals account should be added if the cost is significant.

Total Payroll and Related Expenses

Total Payroll and Related Expenses is the sum of Salaries and Wages, Commissions, Contract, Distributed Service Charges, and Payroll Taxes and Employee Benefits.

Other Expenses

This expense grouping includes significant fitness department expenses. Items appearing under Other Expenses vary from spa to spa. Examples of items that commonly appear as Other Expenses follow.

Ambience. This account includes costs to provide the sensory environment within the fitness department, including background music, cable or satellite television fees, air fresheners, fresh flowers, and similar items.

Athletic Equipment and Supplies. This account includes the cost of athletic supplies, including props for fitness classes, e.g., kick boards for use in lap swimming, jump ropes, volleyball, basketball, racquetball, tennis supplies, or other specialty exercise materials provided to the guest.

Contract Services. This account includes any expenses associated with an activity that is normally charged to fitness, but is now outsourced. Examples include contracting for janitorial or window washing services or maintenance contracts for fitness equipment. This account should not be used for contract instructors, which are recorded in Payroll and Related Expenses—Contract.

Dues and Subscriptions. This account includes the cost of memberships and subscriptions to newspapers and magazines for use by employees in the fitness department.

Equipment Rental. The cost of equipment rented for use in the fitness department should be charged to this account.

Guest Supplies. This account includes the cost of fitness department locker room amenities separate from the spa locker room and supplies provided to the fitness guest on a complimentary basis. Examples would include shampoo, body lotion, razors and shaving cream, etc.

Hospitality. This account includes the costs of bottled water, fresh fruit, juices, herbal teas, coffee and brewing supplies provided to the guest or member in the fitness facility at no cost, plus the cost of service ware including cups, utensils, and napkins.

Laundry. This account includes the cost of processing linens and terry by an outside laundry as determined from bills and invoices sent from outside laundries. In those resort facilities with an in-house laundry, the expense is an allocation of the overall laundry operational costs assigned to the fitness department, which may be determined by the poundage of terry processed for fitness or by the percentage of time devoted to fitness laundry. For small operations that may have their own washers and dryers, the account would be charged for laundry chemicals used to process terry.

Licenses and Fees. This account includes the costs of all state and municipal licenses and permits for the fitness department.

Linen. This account includes the costs of providing towels and any other linen to the fitness department.

Operating Supplies. This is a general account for expenses such as cleaning supplies, printed forms used by the employees, paper supplies such as facial tissue and toilet paper, office supplies, and similar operating expenses in the fitness department.

Professional Development. This account includes costs, other than time, associated with training fitness employees. Examples include the costs of training materials, supplies, instructor's fees, and outside seminars and conferences.

Telecommunications. Any telecommunications expenditures that can be directly related to the fitness department should be charged to this account, such as monthly telephone charges, telephone equipment charges, cell phones, and pagers.

Uniforms. This account includes the cost or rental of uniforms for employees of the fitness department. This expense also includes costs of cleaning and repairing uniforms of fitness employees.

Other. Expenses of the fitness department that do not apply to line items listed or discussed previously are included in this line item.

Total Other Expenses

Total Other Expenses is the sum of all the accounts listed under Other Expenses.

Total Direct Expenses

Total Direct Expenses is the sum of Total Payroll and Related Expenses and Total Other Expenses.

Departmental Income (Loss)

Departmental Income (Loss) is calculated by subtracting Total Direct Expenses from Net Revenue. The Departmental Income (Loss) is the amount that appears on the Summary Statement of Income in the Income (Loss) column for Other Operated Departments—Fitness.

Food and Beverage—Schedule 6

	Current Period
REVENUE	
Food	$
Beverage	
Other Revenue	
TOTAL REVENUE	
ALLOWANCES	
NET REVENUE	
COST OF GOODS SOLD	
Food	
Beverage	
Total Cost of Goods Sold	
GROSS MARGIN	
DIRECT EXPENSES	
Payroll and Related Expenses	
Salaries and Wages	
Payroll Taxes and Employee Benefits	
Total Payroll and Related Expenses	
Other Expenses	
Banquet and Party Costs	
China, Glassware, Silver and Linen	
Contract Services	
Dues and Subscriptions	
Equipment Rental	
Laundry	
Licenses and Fees	
Operating Supplies	
Professional Development	
Telecommunications	
Uniforms	
Utensils	
Other	
Total Other Expenses	
Total Direct Expenses	
DEPARTMENTAL INCOME (LOSS)	$

Food and Beverage—Schedule 6 illustrates a format and identifies line items that commonly appear on a supplemental schedule supporting the amounts reported on the Summary Statement of Income for Other Operated Departments—Food and Beverage. This format and the line items will vary according to the needs and requirements of individual spas, which should modify the schedule to meet their own needs and requirements. Larger spa operations may choose to insert additional revenue categories to further distinguish revenue composition. Smaller spa operations that are unable to collect the information necessary to distribute revenues into the major treatment categories may choose instead to use *Food and*

Beverage—Schedule 6S (short), shown in Section 7. Direct expenses that can be identified for specific operation of the spa department are included on the departmental schedule to determine the contribution of the food and beverage department to the overall spa operation.

There are many food and beverage operations at resort and destination spas that are a department of the overall food and beverage division of the entire facility. In these cases, the "spa café" revenues will be reported on the food and beverage schedules for the property rather than on the spa food and beverage schedule. The basic litmus tests to determine the need for this schedule would be: Is the food and beverage operation with the spa facilities? Does spa management supervise the food and beverage operation? Are the employees of the food and beverage department employees of the spa? Does the revenue generated from food and beverage sales appear on the spa statement of income? If the answers to these questions are no, this is not the appropriate schedule to use.

Revenue

Food

This account includes revenue derived from the sale of food, including coffee, tea, milk, water, and soft drinks, in the spa food and beverage outlet.

Beverage

This account includes revenue derived from the sale of alcoholic beverages in the spa food and beverage outlet. While it is rare, some spas have liquor licenses and sell wine and other alcoholic beverages to spa guests.

Other Revenue

This account includes revenue derived from such sources as rental charges for a private dinner party held on the spa pool deck.

Total Revenue

Total Revenue is the sum of all accounts listed under Revenue.

Allowances

This account includes rebates, refunds, and overcharges of revenue not known at the time of sale but adjusted at a later date.

Net Revenue

Net Revenue is calculated by subtracting Allowances from Total Revenue.

Cost of Goods Sold

Typically, food and beverage are inventoried and reflected on the balance sheet when purchased. Cost of goods sold is calculated by adding total food and/or beverage purchases to the value of the inventory at the beginning of the period and then subtracting the value of inventory at the end of the period. Total food and beverage purchases are each calculated by subtracting trade discounts (but not cash discounts) from the gross invoice price for all food and beverage items and then adding charges for transportation, delivery, and storage. If the policy of the spa facility permits employee sales at cost or a nominal mark-up, the sales should be credited to the Cost of Food or Beverage when they are sold. For those facilities that provide employee meals, the cost of providing meals is charged to Employee Benefits in the departmental Payroll and Related Expenses section. The schedule should show a separate Cost of Goods Sold for food and beverage.

Gross Margin

Gross Margin is calculated by subtracting Total Cost of Goods Sold from Total Revenue.

Direct Expenses

Salaries and Wages

This account includes regular pay, overtime pay, vacation pay, severance pay, holiday pay, and bonuses for employees of the food and beverage department, including those of working supervisors.

Payroll Taxes and Employee Benefits

This account includes payroll taxes, payroll-related insurance expenses, and retirement and other payroll-related expenses applicable to the food and beverage department. In many resort and destination spas, meals are provided to the employees. In these cases, an Employee Meals account should be added if the cost is significant.

Total Payroll and Related Expenses

Total Payroll and Related Expenses is the sum of Salaries and Wages and Payroll Taxes and Employee Benefits.

Other Expenses

This expense grouping includes significant food and beverage department expenses. Items appearing under Other Expenses vary from spa to spa. Examples of items that commonly appear as Other Expenses follow.

Banquet and Party Costs. This account includes miscellaneous expenses associated with private party and banquet revenue such as favors, audio/visual rentals, decorations, and flowers.

China, Glassware, Silver and Linen. This account includes the cost of china, glassware, silver and linen used in the operation of food and beverage service to the spa's guests.

Contract Services. This account includes any expenses associated with an activity that would normally be charged to the food service department, but is outsourced. Examples include the cost of outside companies to wash windows, degrease cooking hoods, and clean carpets and rugs, maintenance of the point-of-sale system and equipment, and contracts to disinfect areas of the food service area.

Dues and Subscriptions. This account should be charged with the cost of memberships in local culinary associations and the cost of newspapers and magazines used by the employees in the spa food and beverage department.

Equipment Rental. This account is charged for rentals such as coffee equipment rental, beverage cooler rental, or soda equipment systems used in the daily operation of the food and beverage department.

Laundry. This account includes any expenses associated with contracting outside laundry services to process linen and uniforms used by the food and beverage department or for a re-bill by the in-house laundry for cost associated with processing the spa food and beverage outlet linens.

Licenses and Fees. This account includes the costs of all federal, state, and municipal licenses for the food and beverage facilities of the spa, including music licenses.

Operating Supplies. This account includes the cost of cleaning supplies, guest supplies, menus, paper supplies, printing and stationery, and similar supplies applicable to the food and beverage department. If the cost of any of these items is significant, items and amounts should be listed separately from operating supplies.

Professional Development. This account includes the costs, other than time, associated with training employees. Examples include the costs of training materials, supplies, and instructor fees.

Telecommunications. Any telecommunications expenditures that can be directly related to the food and beverage department should be charged to this account.

Uniforms. This account includes the cost or rental of uniforms for the employees of the food and beverage department. This account also includes cost of cleaning and repairing uniforms of employees.

Utensils. This account includes the cost of all tools needed in the process of food preparation, such as kitchen knives, whisks, food storage containers, mixing bowls, etc.

Other. Expenses of the food and beverage department that do not apply to accounts discussed previously are included in this line item.

Total Other Expenses

Total Other Expenses is the sum of all the accounts listed under Other Expenses.

Total Direct Expenses

Total Direct Expenses is the sum of Total Payroll and Related Expenses and Total Other Expenses.

Departmental Income (Loss)

Departmental Income (Loss) is calculated by subtracting Total Direct Expenses from Gross Margin. The Departmental Income (Loss) is the amount that appears on the Summary Statement of Income in the Income (Loss) column for Other Operated Departments—Food and Beverage.

Health and Wellness—Schedule 7

	Current Period
Revenue	
Medically Supervised Services	$
Nutrition	
Wellness Consultations	
Wellness Programs	
Breakage	
Service Charges	
Other Revenue	
Total Revenue	
Allowances	
Net Revenue	
Direct Expenses	
Payroll and Related Expenses	
Salaries and Wages	
Commissions	
Contract	
Distributed Service Charges	
Payroll Taxes and Employee Benefits	
Total Payroll and Related Expenses	
Other Expenses	
Contract Services	
Dues and Subscriptions	
Equipment Rental	
Guest Supplies	
Laundry	
Licenses and Fees	
Linen	
Operating Supplies	
Professional Development	
Telecommunications	
Uniforms	
Other	
Total Other Expenses	
Total Direct Expenses	
Departmental Income (Loss)	$

Health and Wellness—Schedule 7 illustrates a format and identifies line items that commonly appear on a supplemental schedule supporting amounts appearing on the Summary Statement of Income for Other Operated Departments—Health and Wellness. The format and line items will vary according to the needs and requirements of individual spas, which should modify the schedule to meet their own needs and requirements. Larger operations may choose to insert additional revenue categories to further distinguish revenue composition. Smaller operations that are unable to collect the information necessary to distribute revenues into the major treatment categories may choose instead to use *Health and Wellness—Schedule 7S* (short), shown in Section 7. Direct expenses that can be identified for specific treatments are included on the departmental schedule to determine the contribution of the health and wellness department to the overall spa operation.

Revenue

Medically Supervised Services

This account includes revenue derived from various types of medically supervised services, including microdermabrasion and photofacials. For medical spas with extensive medical services, it is recommended that a sub-schedule be used to distinguish revenue composition. An example is offered below that shows more revenue categories. The total of the revenues shown on the sub-schedule would be reported under Medically Supervised Services on this schedule.

Nutrition

This account includes revenue derived from consultations and programs conducted by nutrition staff or contractors, including diet analysis, shopping with the nutritionist programs, and healthy cooking demonstration classes.

Wellness Consultations

This account includes revenue derived from various types of wellness consultations, including lifestyle, stress reduction, smoking cessation, or other individual consultations.

Wellness Programs

This account includes revenue derived from various types of group programs conducted by spa staff or contractors dealing with wellness and lifestyle improvements.

Breakage

This account should be charged with any excess of spa packages sold over the retail price of the individual services or unused services included as part of a package or program.

Service Charges

This account should be used to record the total gross service charges collected from the guests for either a fixed amount or a percentage of sale. The distribution of the service charge to employees is charged to the payroll account Distributed Service Charges and is reflected under the Payroll and Related Expenses section of this schedule.

Other Revenue

This account should be used to record revenues from the health and wellness department not identified in the revenue classifications listed.

Total Revenue

Total Revenue is the sum of all accounts listed under Revenue.

Allowances

This account includes rebates, refunds, and overcharges of revenue not known at the time of sale but adjusted at a later date.

Net Revenue

Net Revenue is calculated by subtracting Allowances from Total Revenue.

Direct Expenses

Salaries and Wages

This account includes regular pay, overtime pay, vacation pay, severance pay, holiday pay and bonuses for employees of the health and wellness department, including those of working supervisors.

Commissions

This account includes compensation to health and wellness employees in the form of a percentage commission on services provided.

Contract

This account should be charged with the costs associated with outsourcing health and wellness services, consultations, or programs to independent contractors.

Distributed Service Charges

This account reflects the total amount of service charges paid to the health and wellness employees. Service charges collected from guests are charged to the Service Charge revenue account.

Payroll Taxes and Employee Benefits

This account includes payroll taxes, payroll-related insurance expenses, and retirement, and other payroll-related expenses applicable to the health and wellness department.

Total Payroll and Related Expenses

Total Payroll and Related Expenses is the sum of Salaries and Wages, Commissions, Contract, Distributed Service Charges, and Payroll Taxes and Employee Benefits.

Other Expenses

Contract Services. This account includes any expenses associated with an activity that is normally charged to health and wellness, but is now outsourced. Examples include contracting for janitorial or window washing services or maintenance contracts for fitness equipment. This account should not be used for contract instructors, which are recorded in Payroll and Related Expenses—Contract.

Dues and Subscriptions. This account includes the cost of memberships and subscriptions to newspapers and magazines for use by employees in the health and wellness department.

Equipment Rental. The cost of equipment rented for use in the health and wellness department should be charged to this account.

Guest Supplies. This account includes the cost of amenities provided to the health and wellness guests on a complimentary basis.

Laundry. This account includes the cost of processing linens and terry by an outside laundry as determined from bills and invoices sent from outside laundries. In those resort facilities with an in-house laundry, the expense is an allocation of the overall laundry operational costs assigned to the health and wellness department, which may be determined by the poundage of terry processed for health and wellness or by the percentage of time devoted to health and wellness laundry. For small operations that may have their own washers and dryers, the account would be charged for laundry chemicals used to process terry.

Licenses and Fees. This account includes the costs of all state and municipal licenses and permits for the health and wellness department.

Linen. This account includes the costs of providing towels and any other linen to the health and wellness department.

Operating Supplies. This is a general account for expenses such as cleaning supplies, printed forms used by the employees, paper supplies such as facial tissue and toilet paper, office supplies, and similar operating expenses in the health and wellness department.

Professional Development. This account includes costs, other than employee time, associated with training health and wellness employees. Examples include the costs of training materials, supplies, instructor's fees, and outside seminars and conferences.

Telecommunications. Any telecommunications expenditures that can be directly related to the health and wellness department should be charged to this account, such as monthly telephone charges, telephone equipment charges, cell phones, and pagers.

Uniforms. This account includes the cost or rental of uniforms for employees of the health and wellness department. This expense also includes costs of cleaning and repairing uniforms of health and wellness employees.

Other. Expenses of the health and wellness department that do not apply to line items listed or discussed previously are included in this line item.

Total Other Expenses

Total Other Expenses is the sum of all the accounts listed under Other Expenses.

Total Direct Expenses

Total Direct Expenses is the sum of Total Payroll and Related Expenses and Total Other Expenses.

Departmental Income (Loss)

Departmental Income (Loss) is calculated by subtracting Total Direct Expenses from Gross Margin. The Departmental Income (Loss) is the amount that appears on the Summary Statement of Income in the Income (Loss) column for Other Operated Departments—Health and Wellness.

Sample Sub-Schedule—Medically Supervised Services

	Current Period
Revenue	
Botox	$
Chemical Peels	
Laser Hair Removal	
Medical Esthetics Consultations	
Medical Microdermabrasion	
Photofacials/Intense Pulse Light	
Soft Tissue Fillers—Collagen, Restylane, Perlane	
Total Medically Supervised Revenue	$

Membership Dues and Fees—Schedule 8

	Current Period
REVENUE	
Daily Facility/Guest Fees	$
Initiation Fees	
Membership Dues	
Other Revenue	
TOTAL REVENUE	
ALLOWANCES	
NET REVENUE	$

Membership Dues and Fees—Schedule 8 illustrates a format and identifies line items that commonly appear on a supplemental schedule supporting the amount reported on the Summary Statement of Income for Memberships. This format and line items will vary according to the needs and requirements of individual spas, which should modify Schedule 8 to meet their own needs and requirements. Schedule 8 may not apply to the membership dues and fees structure of every spa.

Revenue

Daily Facility/Guest Fees

This account includes the revenue generated from daily facility fees charged to resort guests, local guests, and the guests of members for the use of the facilities. In the case where a spa has no membership program but does charge a facility fee for the use of the facilities, it is recommended that the Daily Facility/Guest Fees revenues be recorded on *Fitness—Schedule 5* as guests are principally paying the fee for use of the fitness facilities. In those cases where there is a Daily Facility/Guest Fee for spa access, which is waived by resort management but an allocation of rooms revenue is given to the fitness department to underwrite operating costs, it is recommended the allocated revenues be recorded in this line item on the fitness schedule for those spas without a formal membership program.

Initiation Fees

This account includes revenue received for all one-time, non-refundable fees for activating a membership. Initiation fees must be clearly identified as such on the membership agreement. These fees help offset the direct costs associated with obtaining the membership and orienting the new member and are generally recognized when the membership is sold. However, if the profit from initiation fees is material or represents a substantial portion of the overall profit to be earned from a member (from initiation fees, ongoing dues, and service fees), then the initiation fee and associated direct costs shall be deferred and recognized over the weighted average life of the membership rather than at the time the membership is sold (the "deferral method").

The Securities and Exchange Commission has advised public companies operating fitness facilities having initiation fees that they must follow the deferral method of accounting with respect to the revenue recognition and associated costs of initiation fees. Companies that are public or considering becoming public should adopt the deferral method as their method of accounting for initiation fees.

Membership Dues

This account includes revenue received for membership that grant the right to access the spa and the right to basic membership privileges as described in the spa's membership contract/application.

Other Revenue

This account includes revenue from membership dues and fees that have not been discussed previously. Examples include fees for membership category changes, transfer fees, inactive/medical dues for a membership placed on restriction, and fees to cancel a membership before its membership term.

Total Revenue

Total Revenue is the sum of all accounts listed under Revenue.

Allowances

Allowances include rebates, refunds, and over-charges of revenue not known at the time of sale or after an account is billed to the member but adjusted at a later date. An example would be in the case of a disgruntled member, for whom the Spa Director elects to refund a month's dues to placate the member for an unsatisfactory experience.

Net Revenue

Net Revenue is calculated by subtracting Allowances from Total Revenue. Net Revenue is the amount that appears on the Summary Statement of Income for Memberships.

Retail—Schedule 9

	Current Period
Revenue	
Apparel	
Footwear	$
Men's/Unisex	
Robes and Terry	
Women's	
Total Apparel	
Gifts and Accessories	
Books and Media	
Fashion Accessories	
Home	
Total Gifts and Accessories	
Products	
Bath and Body Products	
Hair Products	
Make-up Products	
Nail Products	
Private Label Products	
Skin Care Products	
Total Products	
Other Retail	
Snacks and Beverages	
Sundries	
Other	
Total Other Retail	
Total Revenue	
Revenue Adjustments	
Employee Discounts	
Merchandise Returns	
Allowances	
Total Revenue Adjustments	
Net Revenue	
Cost of Goods Sold	
Gross Margin	
Direct Expenses	
Payroll and Related Expenses	
Salaries and Wages	
Commissions	
Payroll Taxes and Employee Benefits	
Total Payroll and Related Expenses	
Other Expenses	
Buying Trips	
Contract Services	
Dues and Subscriptions	
Equipment Rental	
Gift Wrap and Packaging	
Licenses and Fees	
Merchandise Displays and Accessories	
Merchandise Tags	

Retail—Schedule 9 *(continued)*

	Current Period
Operating Supplies	
Packaging and Freight	
Professional Development	
Telecommunications	
Uniforms	
Other Retail Expenses	
Total Other Expenses	
TOTAL DIRECT EXPENSES	
DEPARTMENTAL INCOME (LOSS)	$

Retail—Schedule 9 illustrates a format and identifies line items that commonly appear on a supplemental schedule supporting amounts appearing on the Summary Statement of Income for Other Operated Departments—Retail. The format and line items will vary according to the needs and requirements of individual spas, which should modify the schedule to meet their own needs and requirements. Larger operations may choose to insert additional revenue categories to further distinguish revenue composition. Operations that are unable to collect the information necessary to distribute revenues into the sub-categories shown should nonetheless use the major classifications, as this will enable sales comparisons to be surveyed industry-wide. Small operations may choose instead to use *Retail—Schedule 9S* (short), shown in Section 7. Direct expenses that can be identified for the retail department are included on the departmental schedule to determine the contribution of the retail department to the overall spa operation.

Revenue

Apparel

Footwear. This account includes revenue deriving from the sale of all footwear, including slippers, sandals, flip-flops, and tennis shoes.

Men's/Unisex. This account includes all sales of men's and unisex apparel, including merchandise such as tee shirts, sweatshirts, sweaters, polo shirts, and sports shirts that would be worn by men or as unisex. Accessories should be charged to the Fashion Accessories account under Gifts and Accessories.

Robes and Terry. This account includes revenue derived from the sale of robes, towels, and other linens.

Women's. This account includes revenue derived from the sale of women's clothing apparel. Accessories should be charged to the Fashion Accessories account under Gifts and Accessories.

Total Apparel. Total Apparel is the sum of all accounts listed under Apparel.

Gifts and Accessories

Books and Media. This account includes revenue from the sale of all books and media, including instructional videos, CDs, DVDs, stationery, books and journals, and note cards.

Fashion Accessories. This account includes revenue derived from the sale of fashion accessories such as jewelry, bags, totes, purses, scarves, hair accessories, and other items that would be considered an accessory to an outfit.

Home. This account includes revenue derived from the sale of home-related gifts such as candles, pillows, throws, pictures, crystal, potpourri, and other decorative items.

Total Gifts and Accessories. Total Gifts and Accessories is the sum of all accounts listed under Gifts and Accessories.

Products

Bath and Body Products. This account includes revenue derived from the sale of bath and body products, accessories, and supplies such as bath salts, oils, soaps, sponges, and after-bath products.

Hair Products. This account includes revenue derived from the sale of hair care products and accessories and supplies.

Make-up Products. This account includes revenue derived from the sale of all make-up-related products, accessories, and supplies. It does not include revenue derived from other facial care products, as they are recorded in the Skin Care Products account.

Nail Products. This account includes revenue derived from the sale of all nail-care-related products, accessories, and supplies.

Private Label Products. This account includes revenue derived from all custom products or signature fragrance products packaged or silk-screened using the spa's own logo or brand.

Skin Care Products. This account includes revenue derived from the sale of various products, accessories, and supplies for care and cleaning of the face, including sun care products. It does not include revenue from the sale of make-up products.

Total Products. Total Products is the sum of all accounts listed under Products.

Other Retail

Snacks and Beverages. This account includes revenue derived from the sale of snacks and beverages such as nutrition bars, bottled waters, teas, and other beverages in the retail area.

Sundries. This account includes revenue derived from the sale of various sundries, including over-the-counter medications, magazines, newspapers, and other personal care items generally sold as a convenience to the guest.

Other. This account includes revenue derived from all other miscellaneous sales such as vitamins and supplements for the retail department.

Total Other Retail. Total Other Retail is the sum of all accounts listed under Other Retail.

Total Revenue

Total Revenue is the sum total of Total Apparel, Total Gifts and Accessories, Total Products, and Total Other Retail.

Revenue Adjustments

Employee Discounts

This account should be charged with any discounts given on goods sold to employees at a discount price. An important financial management practice is to track coupons, gift with purchase and special offers, and other discount programs. Should discounts beyond Employee Discounts be significant, a separate discount account may be added to the retail schedule, which would require reflecting revenues at gross and reducing to net with a discounts account.

Merchandise Returns

This account is charged with all returned goods.

Allowances

This account includes refunds and overcharges of sales not known at the time of the sale but adjusted at a later date.

Total Revenue Adjustments

Total Revenue Adjustments is the sum of Employee Discounts, Merchandise Returns, and Allowances.

Net Revenue

Net Revenue is calculated by subtracting Total Revenue Adjustments from Total Revenue.

Cost of Goods Sold

The direct cost, including tax and freight, of merchandise purchased for resale should be charged to this account. Typically, retail products are inventoried and reflected on the balance sheet when purchased. The reduction of the inventory and cost of sales is then recorded at the point of sale, causing the revenue and related expense to be recorded at the same time. Adjustments to inventory required due to variances between physical inventory counts and the inventory system should also be charged to this account.

Gross Margin

Gross Margin is calculated by subtracting Cost of Goods Sold from Net Revenue.

Direct Expenses

Salaries and Wages

This account includes regular pay, overtime pay, vacation pay, severance pay, holiday pay, and bonuses for employees of the retail department, including those of managers and working supervisors.

Commissions

This account includes compensation to employees in the form of any commissions paid on retail sales or other incentives, regardless of the location of the employee.

Payroll Taxes and Employee Benefits

This account includes payroll taxes, payroll-related insurance expenses, and retirement and other payroll-related expenses applicable to the retail department.

Total Payroll and Related Expenses

Total Payroll and Related Expenses is the sum of Salaries and Wages, Commissions, and Payroll Taxes and Employee Benefits.

Other Expenses

Buying Trips. This account includes all of the costs associated with the retail buyer's travel expenses and registration fees to attend merchandise markets or shows for the purpose of selecting merchandise for the retail department, including any trips to individual suppliers to view new lines.

Contract Services. This account includes any expenses associated with an activity that is normally charged to the retail department, but is now outsourced. Examples would include window washing, carpet cleaning, inventory analysis services, and point-of-sale service contracts.

Dues and Subscriptions. This account includes the cost of memberships and subscriptions to newspapers and magazines for use by employees in the retail department.

Equipment Rental. The cost of equipment rented for use in the retail department should be charged to this account.

Gift Wrap and Packaging. This account includes the cost of shopping bags, wrapping paper, tissue, ribbon, and packaging supplies used in the retail department. It also includes any costs associated with the development of any private label packaging such as design fees or printing.

Licenses and Fees. This account includes the costs of all federal, state, and municipal licenses for the retail facilities of the spa.

Merchandise Displays and Accessories. This account is for all non-capitalized specialty displays or accessories used to enhance the visual appeal of the shop merchandise. Examples would include seasonal or holiday accessories or minor artifacts used on the store fixtures to increase interest.

Merchandise Tags. This account includes the costs associated with pricing retail merchandise.

Operating Supplies. This account includes the cost of cleaning supplies, paper supplies other than gift-wrap or packaging materials, and similar operating expenses applicable to the retail department.

Packaging and Freight. This account is used for any costs associated with shipping retail products to guests, including the costs of packaging materials and mail or shipping charges.

Professional Development. This account includes costs, other than time, associated with training retail employees. Examples include the costs of training materials, supplies, instructor's fees, and outside seminars and conferences.

Telecommunications. Any telephone expenditures that can be directly related to the retail department should be charged to this account. An example would include a specific retail toll-free line for mail order sales.

Uniforms. This account includes the cost or rental of uniforms for the employees of the retail department. This account also includes the cost of cleaning and repairing uniforms of employees.

Other Retail Expenses. This account includes other expenses applicable to the retail department that do not apply to accounts listed above.

Total Other Expenses. Total Other Expenses is the sum of all the accounts listed under Other Expenses.

Total Direct Expenses

Total Direct Expenses the sum of Total Payroll and Related Expenses and Total Other Expenses.

Departmental Income (Loss)

Departmental Income (Loss) is calculated by subtracting Total Direct Expenses from the Gross Margin. Departmental Income (Loss) is the amount that appears on the Summary Statement of Income in the Income (Loss) column for Other Operated Departments—Retail.

Other Operating Departments—Schedule 10

	Current Period
REVENUE	$
ALLOWANCES	
COST OF GOODS SOLD	
GROSS MARGIN	
DIRECT EXPENSES	
Payroll and Related Expenses	
Salaries and Wages	
Payroll Taxes and Employee Benefits	
Total Payroll and Related Expenses	
Other Expenses	
China, Glassware, Silver and Linen	
Contract Services	
Dues and Subscriptions	
Equipment Rental	
Guest Supplies	
Laundry	
Licenses and Fees	
Operating Supplies	
Professional Development	
Telecommunications	
Uniforms	
Other	
Total Other Expenses	
TOTAL DIRECT EXPENSES	
DEPARTMENTAL INCOME (LOSS)	$

Many spas offer services and/or merchandise that are not provided by the operated departments discussed previously. In these cases, spas must decide whether the sale of such services and/or merchandise will be operated by departments within the facility or whether such operations will be contracted through rental or concession agreements. If a facility decides to operate the sale of such services and/or merchandise, a separate schedule should be prepared for each of these areas of operations. Examples of other operated departments are as follows:

- Art Programs
- Adventure Experiences
- Pool/Beach Services
- Children's Camp
- Equestrian
- Guided Hiking Program
- Additional Retail Shops

- Tennis
- Ice Skating

Other Operating Departments—Schedule 10 illustrates a format and identifies line items that commonly appear on a supplemental schedule supporting the Net Revenue, Cost of Sales, Payroll and Related Expenses, Other Expenses, and Departmental Income (Loss) amounts reported on the Summary Statement of Income for Other Operated Departments—Other Operating Departments. The format and line items will vary according to the needs and requirements of individual spas, which should modify the schedule to meet their own needs and requirements.

Revenue

Revenue for any other operating department is derived from the sale of services and/or merchandise applicable to that department. Spas may classify the items appearing under Revenue according to their individual needs and requirements. If, in relation to the total revenue generated by this department, a significant amount of revenue is generated by the sale of an item or by a group of similar items, the item or category should be listed separately under Revenue—Services or under Revenue—Sales of Merchandise.

Allowances

This account include rebates, refunds, and overcharges of revenue not known at the time of sale but adjusted at a later date.

Cost of Goods Sold

The Cost of Goods Sold for other operating departments is calculate by adding the total purchases amount to the value of inventory at the beginning of the period and then subtracting the value of inventory at the end of the period. The total purchases amount is calculated by subtracting the trade discounts (but not cash discounts) from the purchase price of merchandise and then adding transportation and delivery charges.

Gross Margin

This is determined by subtracting Allowances and Cost of Goods Sold from Revenue.

Direct Expenses

Salaries and Wages

This account includes regular pay, overtime pay, vacation pay, sick pay, holiday pay, incentive pay, severance pay, and bonuses for employees of other operating departments. This line item should also include any expense associated with leased labor, but not contract labor, which should be listed separately as Contract Labor under Salaries and Wages as done in the other departments.

Payroll Taxes and Employee Benefits

This account includes payroll taxes, payroll-related insurance expenses, and retirement and other payroll-related expenses applicable to other operating departments.

Total Payroll and Related Expenses

Total Payroll and Related Expenses is the sum of Salaries and Wages and Payroll Taxes and Employee Benefits.

Other Expenses

This expense grouping includes significant expenses of other operating departments. Accounts appearing under Other Expenses vary from facility to facility. Examples of accounts that may appear as Other Expenses include china and glassware, contract services, laundry, guest supplies, operating supplies, professional development, telecommunications, uniforms, and other.

Total Other Expenses

Total Other Expenses is the sum of all accounts listed under Other Expenses.

Total Direct Expenses

Total Direct Expenses is the sum of Total Payroll and Related Expense and Total Other Expenses.

Departmental Income (Loss)

Departmental Income (Loss) is calculated by subtracting Total Direct Expenses from Gross Margin. Departmental Income (Loss) is the amount that appears on the Summary Statement of Income in the Income (Loss) column for Other Operated Departments—Other Operating Departments.

Rentals and Other Income—Schedule 11

	Current Period
Space Rentals and Concessions	$
Cash Discounts Earned	
Cancellation and Unredeemed Gift Certificates	
Foreign Currency Transactions Gains (Losses)	
Interest Income	
Other	
TOTAL RENTALS AND OTHER INCOME	$

Rentals and Other Income—Schedule 11 illustrates a format and identifies line items that commonly appear on a supplemental schedule supporting amounts listed on the Summary Statement of Income for Other Operated Departments—Rentals and Other Income. The format and line items will vary according to the needs and requirements of individual spas, which should modify the schedule to meet their own needs and requirements.

Space Rentals and Concessions

Some spas offer services and/or merchandise to their guests that are not provided by the operating departments previously discussed. In these cases, facilities contract the operations of such activities through rental or concession agreements. This account includes the revenue generated from the rental of space within the facility. The most common examples would include a resort spa renting the salon department to a third party operator or renting space within or adjacent to the spa facility to a physicians group for medically supervised services, renting space to a local restaurant to operate the spa café, and renting retail space to another retail operation or for a feature product line. Separate categories should be used to identify significant revenue items.

Cash Discounts Earned

This account should be credited with the discount earned by the payment of creditors' accounts within the discount period, but should not be credited with trade discounts, which are more properly a deduction from the cost of goods sold.

Cancellation and Unredeemed Gift Certificates

This account should be credited with the income derived from cancellation fees and income from unredeemed gift certificates.

Foreign Currency Transactions Gains (Losses)

This account should include the foreign currency gains or losses from exchanging foreign currency into the local currency of the country that the property uses to report its results of operations.

Interest Income

This account should be credited with interest earned on cash investments, bank deposits, notes receivable, accounts receivable, and other sources.

Other

This account should include items such as commissions not classified under other captions.

Total Rentals and Other Income

Total Rentals and Other Income is the sum of all accounts listed on this schedule. Total Rentals and Other Income is the amount that appears on the Summary Statement of Income in the Income (Loss) column for Other Operated Departments—Rentals and Other Income.

Support Labor—Schedule 12

	Current Period
Salaries and Wages	
Guest Reception	$
Host(ess)/Attendant	
Housekeeping	
Reservations	
Supervision	
Commissions	
Distributed Service Charges	
Payroll Taxes and Employee Benefits	
Total Support Labor	$

Support Labor—Schedule 11 illustrates a format ant identifies line items that commonly appear on a supplemental schedule supporting amounts appearing on the Summary Statement of Income for Indirect Support Labor. The payroll classifications will vary according to the needs and requirements of individual spas. The employees listed on this schedule are not directly involved in the delivery of an individual service, but support the massage, skin care, hair, nail, health and wellness, and in some cases fitness departments. Individual spas should modify Schedule 11 to meet their own needs and requirements.

Salaries and Wages

Guest Reception

This account includes regular pay, overtime pay, vacation pay, severance pay, holiday pay, and bonuses for employees working as guest receptionists. These employees may be called front desk staff, concierge, greeters, valets, and other names for the function of greeting guests and administering guest appointments at the spa.

Host(ess)/Attendant

This account includes regular pay, overtime pay, vacation pay, severance pay, holiday pay, and bonuses for employees working as locker area attendants in resort and destination spas or as host/hostess in a typical day spa facility.

Housekeeping

This account includes regular pay, overtime pay, vacation pay, severance pay, holiday pay, and bonuses for any spa employees whose responsibility it is to perform cleaning services separate from the Host(ess)/Attendant staff. If this function is contracted to an outside service, the expense is recorded on *Schedule 13—Indirect Operating Expenses* under Contract Services.

Reservations

This account includes regular pay, overtime pay, vacation pay, severance pay, holiday pay, and bonuses for any spa employees whose responsibility it is to book advance appointments. Generally this function is performed in a location separate from the guest reception area of the spa or in a central reservations office.

Supervision

This account includes regular pay, overtime pay, vacation pay, severance pay, holiday pay, and bonuses for spa management and working support supervisors. Positions would generally include, for example, Assistant Spa Director, Spa Manager, Front Desk Supervisor, and Lead Attendant. In the case of the Spa Director, resort and destination spas would include this position on this schedule. For day spas, the position of General Manager or Spa Director is recorded on Administrative and General—Schedule 14 under Payroll and Related Expenses—Management Salaries.

Commissions

This account includes compensation to support personnel in the form of a percentage of commissions on treatments sold or other incentive programs.

Distributed Service Charges

This account reflects the total amount of service charge distribution paid to support employees. Service charges distributed to therapists are recorded in the specific department as a Direct Expense—Distributed Service Charges. Service charges collected from guests are charged to the Service Charge revenue line of the relevant department.

Payroll Taxes and Employee Benefits

This account includes payroll taxes, payroll-related insurance expenses, and retirement and other payroll-related expenses applicable to the support personnel. In many resort and destination spa operations, meals are provided to the employees. In these cases, an Employee Meals account should be added if the cost is significant.

Total Support Labor

Total Support Labor is the sum of all of the accounts listed on this schedule. Total Support Labor is the amount that appears on the Summary Statement of Income in the Payroll and Related Expenses column and the Income (Loss) column for Indirect Expenses—Indirect Support Labor.

Indirect Operating Expenses—Schedule 13

	Current Period
Ambience	$
Contract Services	
Dues and Subscriptions	
Equipment Rental	
Guest Clothing	
Guest Supplies	
Hospitality	
Laundry	
Licenses and Fees	
Linen	
Operating Supplies	
Professional Development	
Telecommunications	
Uniforms	
Other	
TOTAL INDIRECT OPERATING EXPENSES	$

Indirect Operating Expenses—Schedule 13 illustrates a format and identifies line items that commonly appear on a supplemental schedule supporting the amounts appearing on the Summary Statement of Income for Indirect Operating Expenses. The expenses identified on this schedule are operating expenses for the spa (that is, one of the four spa departments covered by schedules 1 through 4), but are not specific to an individual spa services department. Guests receiving a spa service or services from one or more of the massage, skin care, hair, or nail departments use the expenses listed on this schedule. The line items listed will vary according to the needs and requirements of individual spas, which should modify the schedule to meet their own needs and requirements.

Indirect Operating Expenses

Ambience

This account includes the costs of providing the sensory environment within a spa, including background music, candles, aromatherapy oils, and diffusers.

Contract Services

This account includes any expenses associated with an activity that is normally charged to the spa, but is outsourced. Examples include the cost of contracting outside companies for janitorial services, window washing, and carpet cleaning.

Dues and Subscriptions

This account is charged with the cost of memberships, such as the International SPA Association and local chamber of commerce, and the cost of subscriptions to newspapers and magazines used by the employees in the spa department (massage, skin care, hair, and nail).

Equipment Rental

The cost of equipment rented for use in the spa should be charged to this account.

Guest Clothing

This account includes the cost of any articles provided and worn by the spa guest, including such items as robes, sandals, workout attire, salon smocks, disposable swim suits or wraps, and turbans.

Guest Supplies

This account includes the cost of the spa locker room area supplies and amenities that are provided on a complimentary basis to spa guests, such as shampoo, body lotion, razors and shaving cream, q-tips and cotton balls, guest-use hair dryers, combs and brushes.

Hospitality

This account includes the costs of bottled water, fresh fruit, juices, herbal teas, coffee, and brewing supplies provided the spa guests at no cost, plus the cost of service-ware including cups, utensils, and napkins.

Laundry

This account includes the cost of processing linens by an outside laundry service as determined from bills and invoices sent from outside laundries. In those resort facilities with an in-house laundry, the expense is an allocation of the overall laundry operational costs assigned to the spa division, which may be determined by the poundage of linen processed for the spa or by the percentage of time devoted to spa laundry. For small operations that may have their own washers and dryers, the account would be charged for laundry chemicals used to process linens.

Licenses and Fees

This account includes the costs of all federal, state, and municipal licenses for the spa facilities, including music licenses.

Linen

This account includes items such as sheets, towels, treatment table covers, blankets, and bath mats used in the spa.

Operating Supplies

This account is a general account for expenses such as cleaning supplies, printed forms used by the employees, paper supplies such as facial tissue and toilet paper, office supplies, and similar operating expenses in the spa, excluding those identifiable supplies used directly in a treatment.

Professional Development

This account includes costs, other than time, associated with training spa employees. Examples include the costs of training materials, supplies, instructor's fees, and outside seminars and conferences.

Telecommunications

Any telecommunications expenditures that can be directly related to the spa should be charged to this account, such as monthly telephone charges, telephone equipment charges, cell-phones, and pagers.

Uniforms

This account includes the cost or rental of uniforms for employees of the spa. This expense also includes costs of cleaning and repairing uniforms of spa employees.

Other

Expenses of the spa division that do not apply to accounts listed or discussed previously are included in this line item.

Total Indirect Operating Expenses

Total Indirect Operating Expenses is the sum of all the accounts on this schedule. Total Indirect Operating Expenses is the amount that appears on the Summary Statement of Income in the Other Expenses column and the Income (Loss) column for Indirect Expenses—Indirect Operating Expenses.

Administrative and General—Schedule 14

	Current Period
Payroll and Related Expenses	
Management Salaries	$
Administrative Salaries and Wages	
Total Salaries and Wages	
Payroll Taxes and Employee Benefits	
Total Payroll and Related Expenses	
Accounting Expenses	
Audit and Other External Expenses	
Payroll Processing Expenses	
Other Accounting Expenses	
Total Accounting Expenses	
Other Expenses	
Bank Charges	
Cash Over/Short	
Contract Services	
Corporate Office Charges	
Credit and Collection	
Credit Card Commissions	
Donations	
Dues and Subscriptions	
Human Resources	
Information Systems	
Legal and Professional	
Licenses and Fees	
Loss and Damage	
Meals and Entertainment	
Operating Supplies	
Postage	
Professional Development	
Provision for Doubtful Accounts	
Security	
Telecommunications	
Travel	
Other	
Total Other Expenses	
Total Administrative and General Expenses	$

Administrative and General—Schedule 14 illustrates a format and identifies line items that commonly appear on a supplemental schedule supporting the Payroll and Related Expenses and Other Expenses amounts appearing on the Summary Statement of Income for Undistributed Operating Expenses—Administrative and General. These expenses are considered applicable to the entire spa operation and not easily allocated to operating departments. For resort and destination spas, the Administrative and General schedule will appear for the entire property and not be included as a schedule for the spa operations, in accordance with the *Uniform System of Accounts for the Lodging Industry,* Ninth Revised Edition, Section

13—Guidelines for Allocating Expenses to Operated Departments (Responsibility Accounting), where departmental income of revenue departments, including spas, is computed by charging against revenues only a limited number of expenses that are traceable to the department. Administrative and General Expenses are an example of this industry standard.

It is recommended that day spas use the format of Undistributed Operating Expenses to record these expenses, which are applicable to the entire spa operation. The format and line items will vary according to the needs and requirements of individual spas, which should modify the schedule to meet their own needs and requirements.

Payroll and Related Expenses

Management Salaries

This account includes salaried exempt employees of the spa operation, plus vacation pay, sick pay, holiday pay, incentive pay, severance pay, and bonuses for management employees of the spa's administrative and general department. For day spas, this account is where the management salaries would be charged. For resort spas, salaries of the Spa Director, Assistant Spa Director, and other salaried exempt spa employees would be recorded on *Support Labor—Schedule 12* under Supervision.

Administrative Salaries and Wages

This account includes regular pay, overtime pay, vacation pay, sick pay, holiday pay, incentive pay, severance pay, and bonuses for support employees of the spa's administrative and general department.

Total Salaries and Wages

Total Salaries and Wages is the sum of Management Salaries and Administrative Salaries and Wages.

Payroll Taxes and Employee Benefits

This account includes payroll taxes, payroll-related insurance expenses, and retirement and other payroll-related expenses applicable to the spa's administrative and general department. If the amount expensed for employee meals is significant, the amount may be disclosed on a separate line titled Employee Meals.

Total Payroll and Related Expenses

Total Payroll and Related Expenses is the sum of Management Salaries, Administrative Salaries and Wages, and Payroll Taxes and Employee Benefits.

Accounting Expenses

Audit and Other External Expenses

This account includes the cost of internal audits billed by the head office, external audits conducted by outside accounting firms, and any service delivery shopper expenses.

Payroll Processing Expenses

All charges from outside parties for processing of payroll are charged to this account.

Other Accounting Expenses

Any accounting expenses that do not apply to accounts discussed previously should be included in this account.

Total Accounting Expenses

Total Accounting Expenses is the sum of all accounts listed under Accounting Expenses.

Other Expenses

Bank Charges

This account includes bank charges assessed for miscellaneous banking services and transactions such as overdrafts, stop payments, check charges, and other related items.

Cash Over/Short

Cashier's overages and shortages are recorded in this account.

Contract Services

This account includes any expense associated with an activity that is normally charged to the administrative and general department, but is outsourced. Examples include the cost of computer and software maintenance contracts and other service contracts related specifically to the administrative and general department. Contracts for security services should be recorded under Security (see below).

Corporate Office Charges

Any portion of administrative salaries and expenses billed to the facility by a corporate office should be charged to this account. The cost of lodging and meals and other applicable services or amenities provided to corporate staff while on business at the facility for the benefit of the facility should also be charged to this account.

Credit and Collection

This account is charged with the cost of collecting guest accounts, including attorney's fees and credit and check verification services.

Credit Card Commissions

This account is charged with the cost of credit card fees.

Donations

Charitable contributions are charged to this account.

Dues and Subscriptions

The cost of representation of the spa, or of members of the staff when authorized to represent the spa, in professional organizations such as ISPA or the local chamber of commerce should be charged to this account. It also should be charged with the costs of subscriptions to newspapers and magazines for use by spa staff (except for those that can be charged directly to a specific department or to indirect operating expenses).

Human Resources

This account includes the cost of recruitment and relocation, printed forms, any employee housing or employee transportation, help wanted advertising, and recruitment/placement fees.

Information Systems

The cost of management information system services, supplies, and equipment (excluding equipment rental and capital items) should be charged to this account. This includes minor equipment, software, supplies, and maintenance.

Legal and Professional

This account should include the cost of any legal fees with respect to a guest claim, trademark or other legal services, and any guest experience shopper expenses.

Licenses and Fees

This account includes the costs of all federal, state, and municipal licenses for the spa facilities, including music licenses, that cannot be charged to a specific department or to indirect operating expenses.

Loss and Damage

Payments made for guest property lost or damaged in excess of the amounts recovered from insurance companies should be charged to this account, as well as settlement of claims for damages.

Meals and Entertainment

This account includes the reimbursable portion of any meal and entertainment expenses incurred by officers of the facility.

Operating Supplies

The cost of general office supplies such as photocopiers, adding machines, calculators, pens and pencils, and other similar equipment and related supplies, excluding equipment rental and capital items, should be charged to this account when used by, or purchased for, departments or employees whose salaries or wages are charged to the administrative and general department.

Postage

This account is charged with the cost of postage, except amounts attributable to marketing the spa.

Professional Development

This account includes costs, other than time, associated with training spa employees that cannot be charged to a specific department or to indirect operating expenses. Examples include the costs of training materials, supplies, instructor's fees, and outside seminars and conferences.

Provision for Doubtful Accounts

A charge adequate to cover the probable loss in collection of accounts receivable is charged to this account.

Security

This account includes the cost of contract security and alarm systems, the cost of transporting bank deposits and change for the spa to a banking institution, and other related expenses.

Telecommunications

Any telecommunications expenditures not identifiable to a single department within the facility or to indirect operating expenses and those directly related to the administrative and general department are charged to this account.

Travel

The cost of travel and reimbursable expenses of employees of the facility traveling on the spa's business is charged to this account, except that traveling in connection with business promotion should be charged to promotion.

Other

Any administrative and general expenses that do not apply to accounts discussed previously should be included in this account.

Total Other Expenses

Total Other Expenses is the sum total of all accounts listed under Other Expenses.

Total Administrative and General Expenses

Total Administrative and General Expenses is the sum of Total Payroll and Related Expenses, Total Accounting Expenses, and Total Other Expenses. Total Administrative and General Expenses is the amount that appears on the Summary Statement of Income in the Income (Loss) column for Undistributed Operating Expenses—Administrative and General.

Marketing—Schedule 15

	Current Period
PAYROLL AND RELATED EXPENSES	
Salaries and Wages	$
Payroll Taxes and Employee Benefits	
Total Payroll and Related Expenses	
OTHER EXPENSES	
Advertising Broadcast	
Advertising Print	
Agency Fees	
Collateral Materials	
Complimentary Guests	
Contract Services	
Direct Mail	
Dues and Subscriptions	
In-House Promotions	
Meals and Entertainment	
Postage	
Professional Development	
Special Events	
Telecommunications	
Trade Shows	
Travel	
Other	
Total Other Expenses	
TOTAL MARKETING EXPENSES	$

Marketing—Schedule 15 illustrates a format and identifies line items that commonly appear on a supplemental schedule supporting the Payroll and Related Expenses and Other Expenses amounts appearing on the Summary Statement of Income for Undistributed Operating Expenses—Marketing. These expenses are considered applicable to the entire spa operation and not easily allocated to operating departments. For resort and destination spas, the marketing schedule will not appear as a separate schedule for spa operations. It will be shown for the entire property. In accordance with the *Uniform System of Accounts for the Lodging Industry*, Ninth Revised Edition, Section 13—Guidelines for Allocating Expenses to Operated Departments is used for charging marketing expenses against revenue departments for a limited number of marketing expenses that are traceable to these departments.

It is recommended that day spas use the format of Undistributed Operating Expenses to record marketing expenses, since they promote revenues in all operating departments of the spa facility. Individual spas should modify the schedule to meet their own needs and requirements.

Payroll and Related Expenses

Salaries and Wages

This account includes regular pay, overtime pay, vacation pay, severance pay, holiday pay, bonuses, and incentives for employees of the marketing department. For day spas, this account is where any marketing employees' salaries and wages would be recorded. For resort and destination spas, the marketing department promotes the entire property, thus any sales and marketing employees would be charged to the resort's marketing expenses. If a resort or destination spa has an employee whose function is to coordinate the spa activities of group attendees or package guests with limited outside sales responsibilities, that employee's salary or wages would appear on *Support Labor—Schedule 12* under Supervision.

Payroll Taxes and Employee Benefits

This account includes payroll taxes, payroll-related insurance expenses, and retirement and other payroll-related expenses applicable to the marketing department.

Total Payroll and Related Expenses

Total Payroll and Related Expenses is the sum of Salaries and Wages and Payroll Taxes and Employee Benefits.

Other Expenses

Advertising Broadcast

This account is charged with the cost of advertising on radio, television, the Internet, and all other non-print forms of advertising, including production costs.

Advertising Print

This account is charged with the cost of advertising placed in newspapers, magazines, and directories, including production costs.

Agency Fees

This account is charged with fees paid to advertising and/or public relations agencies.

Collateral Materials

This account includes the cost of brochures, treatment menus and price sheets, membership kits, and similar materials used to describe the facility's services.

Complimentary Guests

This account is charged with the cost of providing complimentary services that arise from sales and promotional activities.

Contract Services

This account includes any expense associated with an activity that is normally charged to the marketing department, but is outsourced. Examples include equipment maintenance contracts and other service contracts related to advertising and marketing.

Direct Mail

This account includes the cost of mailing lists, printing and postage, envelopes or cards, and other work necessary to large promotional mailings completed in house or by outside direct mail service companies.

Dues and Subscriptions

This account includes the cost of memberships and subscriptions to newspapers and magazines for use by employees in the marketing department.

In-House Promotions

The costs of posters, counter flyers and inserts, tent cards, and similar devices used to stimulate sales within the spa facility should be charged to this account.

Meals and Entertainment

This account includes the reimbursable portion of any meal and entertainment expenses incurred as part of an employee's selling and promotional activities.

Postage

This account includes the cost of postage and shipping attributable to selling activities, excluding postage for large direct mail campaigns.

Professional Development

This account includes costs, other than time, associated with training employees in the marketing department. Examples include the costs of training materials, supplies, and instructor's fees.

Special Events

The costs associated with hosting special events such as familiarization trips, events for journalists, open houses, membership events, and civic parties at the spa designed to generate sales or enhance the public image of the spa are charged to this account.

Telecommunications

Any telecommunication expense that can be directly related to selling activities should be charged to this account.

Trade Shows

This account includes the cost of promoting the spa at various trade shows, including the travel and subsistence expenses of attending representatives, cost of booths or displays, promotional logo items, and rental of exhibition space.

Travel

This account includes the cost of transportation and reimbursable travel expenses of employees and officers engaged in sales promotion and the cost of entertainment for the purpose of promoting business.

Other

This account includes all marketing expenses not discussed previously, including such items as the cost of analyzing guest history data or research prepared by independent research or consulting firms in order to determine the demographic or geographic characteristics of the spa's business; photography used in various types of promotional and publicity programs, including professional models; and similar miscellaneous costs in maintaining the public image of the spa. Franchise fees should also be included in this account unless they are significant, in which case they should be disclosed on a separate line. Franchise fees include all fees charged to the franchise company, including royalties, fees for national advertising, and fees associated with the administration of frequent guest programs.

Total Other Expenses

Total Other Expenses is the sum of all Other Expenses.

Total Marketing Expenses

Total Marketing Expenses is the sum of Total Payroll and Related Expenses and Total Other Expenses. Total Marketing Expenses is the amount that appears on the Summary Statement of Income in the Income (Loss) column for Undistributed Operating Expenses—Marketing.

Facility Maintenance and Utilities—Schedule 16

	Current Period
PAYROLL AND RELATED EXPENSES	
Salaries and Wages	$
Payroll Taxes and Employee Benefits	________
Total Payroll and Related Expenses	________
OTHER EXPENSES	
Facility Maintenance Expenses	
Building	
Contract Services	
Dues and Subscriptions	
Equipment Rental	
Equipment Repair	
Grounds and Landscaping	
Heating, Ventilating, and Air Conditioning	
Licenses and Fees	
Locks and Keys	
Operating Supplies	
Sauna, Steam, and Pool Supplies and Repairs	
Trash Removal	
Uniforms	
Other Repairs and Maintenance	________
Total Facility Maintenance Expenses	________
Utility Expenses	
Electric	
Gas	
Water	
Other Fuels	________
Total Utility Expenses	________
TOTAL OTHER EXPENSES	________
TOTAL FACILITY MAINTENANCE AND UTILITIES EXPENSES	$ ________

Facility Maintenance and Utilities—Schedule 16 illustrates a format and identifies line items that commonly appear on a supplemental schedule supporting the amount reported on the Summary Statement of Income under Undistributed Operating Expenses—Facility Maintenance and Utilities. This format and the line items will vary according to the needs and requirements of individual spas. In the case of resort and destination spas with overnight accommodations, the expenses reflected on this supplemental schedule would be charged to the property's Undistributed Operating Expenses in accordance with the *Uniform System of Accounts for the Lodging Industry,* Section 13—Guidelines for Allocating Expenses to Operated Departments (Responsibility Accounting). The lodging industry has determined that the departmental income of the revenue departments (e.g., rooms, food and beverage, and other departments, including spa) is computed by charging against revenues only a limited number of expenses that are traceable to the department. Undistributed Operating Expenses such as marketing, facility maintenance and utilities, and rent, insurance, and property taxes are not charged against revenue departments. This measurement approach to departmental income is chosen to help ensure account uniformity. Uniformity is important for the comparability of operating units. It may be necessary to ascribe many of the undistributed operating expenses and deductions from gross operating profit to the revenue departments to have a complete measure of departmental performance. If assigning these costs is deemed to be valuable to management for decision-making, it should be done in accordance with Section 13 of the *Uniform System of Accounts for the Lodging Industry,* Ninth Revised Edition (or the corresponding section of any subsequent edition). The line items listed on Schedule 16 may not apply to the facility maintenance and utilities of every spa. Individual spa operations should modify Schedule 16 to meet their own needs and requirements.

Payroll and Related Expenses

Salaries and Wages

This account includes regular pay, overtime pay, vacation pay, severance pay, holiday pay, and bonuses for employees of the facility maintenance department. This account does not include payments to independent contractors, which should be charged to Contract Services.

Payroll Taxes and Employee Benefits

This account includes payroll taxes, payroll-related insurance expenses, and retirement and other payroll-related expenses applicable to the facility maintenance department.

Total Payroll and Related Expenses

Total Payroll and Related Expenses is the sum of Salaries and Wages and Payroll Taxes and Employee Benefits.

Other Expenses

Facility Maintenance Expenses

Building. This account includes the cost of materials and contracts related to the repair and maintenance of the spa building, both exterior and interior. Examples would include repairs to the roof, ceilings, walls, windows, sidewalks, parking lots, and stairways.

Contract Services. This account is charged for any expenses related to maintaining the facility that are outsourced and not specifically identified elsewhere. Examples would include elevator maintenance and inspection contracts and pest control service contracts.

Dues and Subscriptions. This account includes the cost of memberships and subscriptions to newspapers and magazines for use by employees in the facilities maintenance department.

Equipment Rental. This account includes the cost of equipment rented for use by the facility maintenance department.

Equipment Repair. This account is charged with the cost of materials and contracts related to repairing and maintaining general equipment not specifically identified elsewhere. Examples would include general electrical and mechanical equipment, laundry equipment, refrigeration equipment, and water softeners. Maintenance contracts for specialized equipment such as hydrotherapy tubs, cardio equipment, and data processing should be charged directly to the appropriate department Contract Services expense.

Grounds and Landscaping. This account includes the cost of supplies and contracts related to the maintenance of the grounds.

Heating, Ventilating, and Air Conditioning. This account is charged with the cost of materials and contracts related to repairing all heating, ventilating, and air conditioning equipment.

Licenses and Fees. This account includes the costs of all federal, state, and municipal licenses for the maintenance of facilities.

Locks and Keys. This account is charged with the cost of materials and repairs for lockers and keys, safe deposit boxes, and general facility door hardware and panic hardware, safes, etc.

Operating Supplies. The cost of general supplies to maintain the facility such as (for example) light bulbs, small tools, painting supplies, toilet parts, showerhead replacement, and upholstery fabric is charged to this account.

Sauna, Steam, and Pool Supplies and Repairs. This account is charged with the cost of materials, chemicals, supplies, and contracts relating to the maintenance and repair of swimming pools, whirlpools, saunas, and steam rooms.

Trash Removal. The cost of the removal of rubbish and any hazardous materials is charged to this account.

Uniforms. This account includes the cost or rental of uniforms for the employees of the facility maintenance department. This account also includes the costs of cleaning and repairing uniforms of employees.

Other Repairs and Maintenance. This account includes all facility maintenance expenses not discussed previously. If any expense is significant, it should be separately disclosed.

Total Facility Maintenance Expenses. Total Facility Maintenance Expenses is the sum of all the accounts listed under Facility Maintenance Expenses.

Utility Expenses

Electric. The cost of light and power from the local utility company is charged to this account.

Gas. This account includes the cost of fuel consumed, including heating fuel, natural gas, and propane gas.

Water. This account is charged with the cost of water used, including costs associated with treating water with specialty equipment.

Other Fuels. The cost of other fuels such as geothermal, steam, or fuel oil is charged to this account. If the cost of any other fuels is significant, a separate line should be used.

Total Utility Expenses. Total Utility Expenses is the sum of all the accounts listed under Utility Expenses.

Total Other Expenses

Total Other Expenses is the sum of Total Facility Maintenance Expenses and Total Utility Expenses.

Total Facility Maintenance and Utilities Expenses

Total Facility Maintenance and Utilities Expenses is the sum of Total Payroll and Related Expenses and Total Other Expenses. This is the same amount that appears on the Summary Statement of Income under Undistributed Operating Expenses—Facility Maintenance and Utilities.

Fixed Charges—Schedule 17

	Current Period
RENT	
Land and Buildings	$
Other Equipment	
Total Rent Expense	
TAXES OTHER THAN INCOME AND PAYROLL	
Real Estate Taxes	
Personal Property Taxes	
Business and Occupation Taxes	
Total Taxes Other than Income and Payroll	
INSURANCE	
Building and Improvements	
Liability	
Total Insurance	
MANAGEMENT FEES	
TOTAL FIXED CHARGES	$
DEPRECIATION AND AMORTIZATION	
Building and Improvements	
Furnishings and Equipment	
Leaseholds and Leasehold Improvements	
Capital Leases	
Other	
Total Depreciation and Amortization	$
INTEREST EXPENSE	
Mortgages	
Notes Payable	
Interest on Capital Leases	
Other Long-term Debt	
Other	
Total Interest Expense	$
(GAIN) LOSS ON DISPOSAL OF PROPERTY	$

Fixed Charges—Schedule 17 illustrates a format and identifies line items that commonly appear on a supplemental schedule supporting the following items reported on the Summary Statement of Income: Fixed Charges, Depreciation and Amortization, Interest Expense, and Gain or Loss on Disposal of Property. This format and line items will vary according to the needs and requirements of individual spas, which should modify the schedule to meet their own needs and requirements. Resort and destination spas report fixed charges for the overall property on the resort's consolidated Statement of Income.

Rent

Land and Buildings

This account includes the rental cost (both face or minimum and percentage rent) of the spa facility.

Other Equipment

This account includes the cost of other items leased or rented and used by the spa for the benefit of the entire facility. An example would be vehicle rental. Equipment leased or rented is included under Indirect Operating Expenses for the treatment departments and individually in the other operated departments. In the case of resort and destination spas, the *Uniform System of Accounts for the Lodging Industry,* Ninth Revised Edition, treats all leases and rentals as a fixed charge and does not charge the cost of leases to the operating departments.

Total Rent Expense

Total Rent Expense is the sum of all accounts listed under Rent.

Taxes Other than Income and Payroll

Real Estate Taxes

This account includes all taxes assessed against the real property of the spa by a state or political subdivision of a state, such as county or city.

Personal Property Taxes

This account includes personal property taxes on furnishings, fixtures, and equipment.

Business and Occupation Taxes

This account includes taxes that cannot be passed on to guests, such as annual business filing fees, gross receipt taxes, and other taxes that have not been discussed previously.

Total Taxes Other than Income and Payroll

Total Taxes Other than Income and Payroll is the sum of all accounts listed under Taxes Other than Income and Payroll.

Insurance

Building and Improvements

This account includes the cost of insuring the facility building and contents against damage or destruction by fire, weather, sprinkler leakage, boiler explosion, plate glass breakage, or any other cause.

Liability

General insurance costs, including premiums relating to liability, fidelity, and theft coverage, are charged to this account. Payroll-related insurance (workers' compensation) is included in Employee Benefits in the appropriate departmental schedule to which the associated payroll is charged.

Total Insurance

Total Insurance is the sum of all accounts listed under Insurance.

Management Fees

This account includes the cost of base fees and any incentive fees of an independent management company to operate the spa.

Total Fixed Charges

Total Fixed Charges is the sum of the accounts listed above.

Depreciation and Amortization

Building and Improvements

Depreciation on the facility's buildings and improvements is charged to this account over their estimated useful lives.

Furnishings and Equipment

This account includes depreciation of furnishings and equipment over their estimated useful lives. This account should include deprecation of computer and office equipment, treatment equipment, exercise equipment, etc.

Leaseholds and Leasehold Improvements

This account includes the amortization of costs associated with acquiring leaseholds. These costs are amortized over the life of the related lease. This account also includes the amortization of costs associated with leasehold improvements. These costs are amortized over the life of the related lease or the life of the improvements, whichever is shorter.

Capital Leases

This account includes the depreciation of assets held under capital leases.

Other

This account includes the amortization of intangible assets, the amortization of capitalized pre-opening expenditures, and the depreciation of fixed assets that do not apply to accounts discussed previously.

Total Depreciation and Amortization

Total Depreciation and Amortization is the sum of all of the accounts under Depreciation and Amortization.

Interest Expense

This account group includes interest expense on all obligations such as mortgages, notes payable, bonds, debentures, taxes in arrears, or any other indebtedness on which interest is charged. This account also includes the portion of capital lease payments that represents interest on the obligations under capital leases. Interest Expense also includes amortization of deferred financing and other costs associated with obtaining financing. Items reported under Interest Expense should be listed by categories that indicate the source of the principal indebtedness on which interest is incurred.

(Gain) Loss on the Disposal of Property

This account lists separately significant gains or losses on the disposal of property and equipment.

Federal and State Income Taxes—Schedule 18

	Current Period
FEDERAL	
Current	$
Deferred	
Total Federal	
STATE	
Current	
Deferred	
Total State	
TOTAL FEDERAL AND STATE INCOME TAXES	$

All taxes that are assessed on the basis of income earned by the spa should be charged to the accounts shown on *Federal and State Income Taxes—Schedule 18.* When there are differences between income reported for financial statement purposes and income reported for income tax purposes, the amount of income tax currently payable and the amount that has been deferred should be shown separately. Items that give rise to deferred income taxes include, but are not limited to, the difference in tax and book depreciation and items capitalized as property and equipment on the books but treated as an expense for tax purposes.

The Total Federal and State Income Taxes is the amount that appears on the Summary Statement of Income (Loss) for Income Taxes.

Payroll Taxes and Employee Benefits—Schedule 19

	Current Period
PAYROLL TAXES	
Federal Retirement (FICA)	$
Federal Unemployment (FUTA)	
Medicare (FICA)	
State Disability	
State Unemployment (SUTA)	
Total Payroll Taxes	
EMPLOYEE BENEFITS	
Auto Allowance	
Child Care	
Contributory Savings Plan (401k)	
Dental Insurance	
Disability Pay	
Group Life Insurance	
Health Insurance	
Meals	
Profit Sharing	
Stock Benefits	
Workers' Compensation	
Other	
Total Employee Benefits	
TOTAL PAYROLL TAXES AND EMPLOYEE BENEFITS	$
CHARGED TO	
Massage	
Skin Care	
Hair	
Nail	
Food and Beverage	
Health and Wellness	
Indirect Support Labor	
Retail	
Administrative and General	
Marketing	
Facility Maintenance and Utilities	
Other Operating Activities	

Payroll Taxes and Employee Benefits—Schedule 19 illustrates a format and identifies line items that commonly appear in various departments under Payroll and Related Expenses. This format and the line items will vary according to the needs and requirements of individual operations. For larger operations, it is acceptable to add additional expense categories to further distinguish expense composition. Individual spas should modify the schedule to meet their own needs and requirements. All costs associated with these items should be expensed to *Payroll Taxes and Employee Benefits—Schedule 19,* then allocated based on percentage of payroll to each department listed. An alternative is to expense these costs directly to the individual departments, therefore minimizing the need for this schedule.

Payroll Taxes

Federal Retirement (FICA)

This account is charged with taxes imposed on employers.

Federal Unemployment (FUTA)

This account is charged with taxes imposed by Chapter 23 of the Internal Revenue Code.

Medicare (FICA)

This account is charged with taxes imposed on employers by Subchapter B, Chapter 21, of the Internal Revenue Code.

State Disability

This account is charged with employer contributions to state agencies for disability purposes.

State Unemployment (SUTA)

This account is charged with contributions to state unemployment funds as required by state law.

Total Payroll Taxes

Total Payroll Taxes is the sum of all items listed under Payroll Taxes.

Employee Benefits

Auto Allowance

This account is charged with the cost of providing payment to employees for company-owned vehicles and allowances for use of autos.

Child Care

This account is charged with the cost of providing contracted care or in-house facilities for employees' children.

Contributory Savings Plan (401k)

The employer's portion of matching and administrative costs of the savings program is charged to this account.

Dental Insurance

This account is charged with the employer's cost of dental insurance for employees less amounts reimbursed.

Disability Pay

This account is charged with the cost of providing disability pay to employees.

Group Life Insurance

This account is charged with the cost of group life insurance on employees.

Health Insurance

This account is charged with the employer's cost of health insurance for employees less amounts reimbursed.

Meals

This account is charged with the cost associated with providing meals to employees.

Profit Sharing

This account is charged with the cost of the employer's contribution to a profit sharing plan.

Stock Benefits

This account is charged with the cost of providing employees with company stock.

Workers' Compensation

This account is charged with the employer's cost of insurance for employee state compensation plans.

Other

This account is charged with the cost of other employee benefits not listed above (e.g., name tags, employee award and incentive parties, etc.).

Total Employee Benefits

Total Employee Benefits is the sum of all accounts listed under Employee Benefits.

Total Payroll Taxes and Employee Benefits

Total Payroll Taxes and Employee Benefits is the sum of Total Payroll Taxes and Total Employee Benefits.

Section 7
Short Versions of Departmental Statements

Section 6 contains the Summary Statement of Income and 19 schedules. For some smaller spas, the Summary Statement and 19 schedules may contain considerably more detail than their operators desire. This section contains short versions of many of the schedules in Section 6. The numbers for the short versions in this section match the numbers in Section 6, but are distinguished by an added "S" signifying "short." For example, the Massage Schedule in Section 6 is Schedule 1, while the Message Schedule in this section is Schedule 1S. These schedules may be modified to suit the needs of the smaller spa operator. A number of the schedules in Section 6 do not have short versions. For schedules 8, 11, 12, 13, 18, and 19, the short version would be identical to the version in Section 6. For that reason, those schedules are not duplicated here.

Summary Statement of Income (Short Format)

	Schedule	Net Revenue	Cost of Sales	Payroll and Related Expenses	Other Expenses	Income (Loss)
TOTAL SPA CONTRIBUTIONS	1, 2, 3, 4	$	$	$	$	$
TOTAL INDIRECT EXPENSES	12, 13					
SPA AFTER INDIRECT EXPENSES						
MEMBERSHIPS	8					
TOTAL OTHER OPERATED DEPARTMENTAL CONTRIBUTIONS	5, 6, 7, 9, 10, 11					
INCOME BEFORE UNDISTRIBUTED EXPENSES						
UNDISTRIBUTED OPERATING EXPENSES	14, 15, 16					
INCOME BEFORE FIXED CHARGES		$	$	$	$	
FIXED CHARGES	17					
INCOME BEFORE DEPRECIATION, AMORTIZATION, INTEREST AND INCOME TAXES						
DEPRECIATION AND AMORTIZATION	17					
INTEREST EXPENSE	17					
GAIN OR LOSS ON DISPOSAL OF PROPERTY	17					
INCOME BEFORE INCOME TAXES						
INCOME TAXES	18					
NET INCOME						$

Massage—Schedule 1S

REVENUE	
Massage	$
Body Treatments	
Other	______
TOTAL REVENUE	
ALLOWANCES	______
NET REVENUE	
DIRECT EXPENSES	
Payroll and Related Expenses	
Other Expenses	______
TOTAL DIRECT EXPENSES	______
DEPARTMENTAL CONTRIBUTION	$ ______

Skin Care—Schedule 2S

REVENUE	
Facial Treatments	$
Waxing Services	
Other	______
TOTAL REVENUE	
ALLOWANCES	______
NET REVENUE	
DIRECT EXPENSES	
Payroll and Related Expenses	
Other Expenses	______
TOTAL DIRECT EXPENSES	______
DEPARTMENTAL CONTRIBUTION	$ ______

Hair—Schedule 3S

REVENUE	
Color and Chemical	$
Styling	
Other	______
TOTAL REVENUE	
ALLOWANCES	______
NET REVENUE	
DIRECT EXPENSES	
Payroll and Related Expenses	
Other Expenses	______
TOTAL DIRECT EXPENSES	______
DEPARTMENTAL CONTRIBUTION	$ ______

Nail—Schedule 4S

REVENUE	
Manicure	$
Pedicure	
Other	______
TOTAL REVENUE	
ALLOWANCES	______
NET REVENUE	
DIRECT EXPENSES	
Payroll and Related Expenses	
Other Expenses	______
TOTAL DIRECT EXPENSES	______
DEPARTMENTAL CONTRIBUTION	$ ______

Fitness—Schedule 5S

REVENUE	
Personal Training	$
Group Exercise	
Fitness Evaluations	
Other Revenue	______
TOTAL REVENUE	
ALLOWANCES	______
NET REVENUE	
DIRECT EXPENSES	
Payroll and Related Expenses	
Other Expenses	______
TOTAL DIRECT EXPENSES	______
DEPARTMENTAL INCOME (LOSS)	$ ______

Food and Beverage—Schedule 6S

REVENUE	
Food	$
Beverage	
Other Revenue	______
TOTAL REVENUE	
ALLOWANCES	______
NET REVENUE	
COST OF GOODS SOLD	______
GROSS MARGIN	
DIRECT EXPENSES	
Payroll and Related Expenses	
Other Expenses	______
TOTAL DIRECT EXPENSES	______
DEPARTMENTAL INCOME (LOSS)	$ ______

Health and Wellness—Schedule 7S

REVENUE	
Medically Supervised Services	$
Nutrition	
Wellness Consultations	
Wellness Programs	
Other Revenue	
TOTAL REVENUE	
ALLOWANCES	
NET REVENUE	
DIRECT EXPENSES	
Payroll and Related Expenses	
Other Expenses	
TOTAL DIRECT EXPENSES	
DEPARTMENTAL INCOME (LOSS)	$

Retail—Schedule 9S

REVENUE	
Apparel	$
Gifts and Accessories	
Products	
Other Revenue	
TOTAL REVENUE	
REVENUE ADJUSTMENTS	
NET REVENUE	
COST OF GOODS SOLD	
GROSS MARGIN	
DIRECT EXPENSES	
Payroll and Related Expenses	
Other Expenses	
TOTAL DIRECT EXPENSES	
DEPARTMENTAL INCOME (LOSS)	$

Other Operating Departments—Schedule 10S

REVENUE	$
ALLOWANCES	
COST OF GOODS SOLD	______
GROSS MARGIN	
DIRECT EXPENSES	
Payroll and Related Expenses	
Other Expenses	______
TOTAL DIRECT EXPENSES	______
DEPARTMENTAL INCOME (LOSS)	$ ______

Administrative and General—Schedule 14S

PAYROLL AND RELATED EXPENSES	$
ACCOUNTING EXPENSES	
OTHER EXPENSES	______
TOTAL ADMINISTRATIVE AND GENERAL EXPENSES	$ ______

Marketing—Schedule 15S

PAYROLL AND RELATED EXPENSES	$
OTHER EXPENSES	______
TOTAL MARKETING EXPENSES	$ ______

Facility Maintenance and Utilties—Schedule 16S

TOTAL PAYROLL AND RELATED EXPENSES	$
TOTAL FACILITY MAINTENANCE EXPENSES	
TOTAL UTILITIES	______
TOTAL FACILITY MAINTENANCE AND UTILITIES EXPENSES	$ ______

Fixed Charges—Schedule 17S

RENT	$
TAXES OTHER THAN INCOME AND PAYROLL	
INSURANCE	
MANAGEMENT FEES	
INTEREST EXPENSE	
DEPRECIATION AND AMORTIZATION	
(GAIN) LOSS ON SALE OF PROPERTY	______
TOTAL EXPENSES	$ ______

Part II
Financial Analysis

Section 8
Financial Statement Formats

The formats of the Statement of Income and departmental schedules can be designed to provide only one amount column to record figures for the time period covered by the statement. While the primary purpose of any of these statements is to present the revenue and expenses for the most recent accounting period, the true significance of such amounts can be fully understood only when compared with budgets and/or the corresponding amounts for preceding periods. Accordingly, an individual spa should modify the format of these statements to meet its needs and requirements. For example, spas may find it useful to expand this basic format by adding columns to provide:

- A comparative analysis of the current period results with the amounts budgeted for the period
- A comparative analysis of the current period results with those of the same period for the preceding year
- Cumulative year-to-date information
- Percentage relationships between revenue and expenses

Comparisons can be made by either horizontal or vertical analyses. Horizontal analysis indicates the absolute (dollar) and relative (percentage) differences between the two amounts of the same line items. The absolute differences are simply the dollar differences between the figures (this year and last year or actual and budget). The relative differences are percentage differences, and are calculated by dividing the absolute differences by the prior year or budget amounts. Vertical analysis uses net revenue as a common denominator and reduces the amount of each line on the respective income statements to a percentage. This analysis produces common-size statements that permit reasonable comparisons of two or more periods with different levels of activity.

The widespread use of spreadsheet programs and personal computers has greatly facilitated the generation of more complex income statement formats. The user need only enter current and prior period or budget information, and the computer can perform the necessary computations and format the statements.

Alternative Income Statement Format A presents a format that includes columns for both current period and year-to-date information and comparative figures. The comparative figures may be budget numbers or the results of the same period for the preceding year. A comparison to budget or forecast is preferred since this enables management to concentrate on the underlying business reasons that actual results exceeded or fell short of planned results. Comparisons with previous periods, although not as meaningful as comparisons with budgets, are useful for indicating the relative performance of current operations.

For those spas desiring a more complete presentation, *Alternative Income Statement Format B* includes a provision for both current period and year-to-date information as well as for comparison with both the budget and a prior period. In addition, a column has been provided to show the current month and year-to-date dollar variance between actual results and the budget. In this instance, an explanatory analysis of the variance should accompany the financial statements.

When calculating the percentage columns of these alternative income statements, net revenue is normally used as the base and expenses are expressed as a percentage of net revenue. Spas may choose to show the percentages for all line items or only those for the more important items. In addition to reporting the percentage relationship between revenue and expenses, departmental schedules may also present statistical information regarding the efficiency of operations. Typical statistics are discussed in Section 9.

Alternative Income Statement Format A

Acct. No.	Line Item Description	Current Month				Year-To-Date			
		Actual		Comparative		Actual		Comparative	
		Dollars	Percent	Dollars	Percent	Dollars	Percent	Dollars	Percent

Alternative Income Statement Format B

Current Month							Acct. No.	Line Item Description	Year-To-Date						
Actual		Budget			Prior Year				Actual		Budget			Prior Year	
Dollars	Percent	Dollars	Percent	Variance	Dollars	Percent			Dollars	Percent	Dollars	Percent	Variance	Dollars	Percent

Section 9
Ratio Analysis and Statistics

The use of ratios and statistics as a basis of comparison, measurement, and communication is prevalent within the spa industry. There are many useful ratios that can be calculated, but their usefulness in comparing one spa with other spas is predicated on common definitions. The intent of this section is to provide a uniform definition of basic industry ratios and statistics. This section focuses on ratios and statistics that are commonly used within the industry. It is *not* a complete listing of all possible relevant ratios and statistics.

Financial statements contain a significant amount of information, and thorough analysis of this information can yield meaningful insight into a spa's operational results and financial position. This is accomplished through ratio analysis, which compares related facts reported on financial statements. A ratio gives mathematical expression to a relationship between two figures and is calculated by dividing one figure by the other.

Comparison Benchmarks

Although ratios are critical to any financial analysis, they are only indicators, and as indicators, they are meaningful only when compared with useful criteria known as benchmarks. Benchmarks with which to compare the results of ratio analysis include:

- The ratios of other spas and industry averages
- Spa-specific historical ratios (time series analysis comparing ratios from more than one period)
- Spa-specific ratio goals

When compared with desired benchmarks, ratios can be extremely useful. However, ratios do not in themselves resolve financial problems. Rather, when ratios vary significantly from past periods, budgeted standards, or industry averages, they indicate that problems or inefficiencies *may* exist. When significant variances exist, additional analysis and investigation is necessary to determine their causes and, if necessary, the appropriate corrective actions.

The comparison of financial performance measurements with those of other facilities and industry averages can be valuable. However, care must be used when comparing the performance of one spa's operation with the performance of the industry, a competing set of spas, or a comparable group or type of spa. Points to consider include the following:

- The performance of the subject spa should be measured against facilities of similar size, age, location, revenue mix, market mix, branding, ownership structure, management, facilities and services offered, amenities offered, etc. Careful consideration should be given to the comparability of these criteria and the degree to which the criteria influence financial performance.

- When comparing the subject ratios to the benchmarks, understand that there may be valid reasons a particular spa achieves a performance level above or below the benchmark. Significant benchmark variances simply indicate the need for further investigation.
- Industry or sub-group benchmarks from other spas are averages and may not represent optimal performance. You may attempt to exceed the benchmark profit levels.

While comparison to an industry-wide competitive set or comparable facility has some use for benchmarking of a spa, an internal analysis of a spa's operation from period to period or against budget is an invaluable practice. This discipline can provide insight to:

- Changes in revenues and expenses from period to period
- Correlations between revenues, expenses, and treatments performed
- Individual department efficiencies
- Performance against budgeted goals

There are various ways to analyze ratios and compare statistics. The proper method used is often dictated by the fixed or variable nature of the revenue or expense item. In general, fixed revenues and expenses remain unaffected in the short term (generally one year) by changes in operating volumes. Examples of fixed expenses are property/liability insurance, property taxes, and management fees. Examples of fixed revenue could be rental payments from a retail operation leasing space or salon chair and treatment room rentals.

Variable revenues and expenses are those that are driven by business volume. In this industry, volumes are predominantly measured by the number of treatments given. Variable expenses closely tied to the number of services performed would include employee commissions, laundry, and operating supplies. Some expenses vary directly with changes in revenue—franchise fees and therapist commission payroll are two examples.

Some revenue and expense items have both fixed and variable components—for instance, a rental fee comprising a base fee per month plus an additional payment based on sales. Another example would be a therapist who is paid a base salary as well as a commission on services. The base rent and base salary are fixed expenses, while the sales-based rental payment and the commission payments are variable expenses based on business volume.

Liquidity Ratios

Liquidity ratios measure an operation's ability to meet its short-term (less than one year) obligations. Owners and stockholders often prefer relatively low liquidity ratios because investments in current assets may be less productive than investments in noncurrent assets. Creditors, on the other hand, normally prefer high liquidity ratios because high ratios give them assurance that the spa will be able to meet its short-term obligations. Management must try to balance the needs of owners and creditors while maintaining adequate working capital and sufficient liquidity to ensure the efficient operation of the spa.

Current Ratio

The most common liquidity ratio is the current ratio, which is calculated as follows:

$$\text{Current Ratio} = \frac{\text{Current Assets}}{\text{Current Liabilities}}$$

Assume, for example, that *Any Spa* has current assets of $350,000 and current liabilities of $300,000. *Any Spa's* current ratio is $350,000 ÷ $300,000, or 1.167. This ratio reveals that for every $1 of current liabilities, *Any Spa* has $1.17 to pay those liabilities.

Acid-Test Ratio

The acid-test ratio measures a spa's liquidity by considering only "quick assets," which are current assets minus inventories and prepaid expenses. This is often a more stringent measure of a property's liquidity because it may take several months to convert inventories to cash. The acid-test ratio is calculated as follows:

$$\text{Acid-Test Ratio} = \frac{\text{Quick Assets}}{\text{Current Liabilities}}$$

If *Any Spa* has quick assets of $225,000 and current liabilities of $300,000, its acid-test ratio is $225,000 ÷ $300,000, or .75. This ratio reveals that for every $1 of current liabilities, *Any Spa* has approximately $ .75 to pay those liabilities.

Accounts Receivable Turnover

Accounts receivable is often the largest current asset of resort and destination spas because of credit provisions provided to guests. Therefore, any examination of a spa's liquidity must consider how quickly accounts receivable are converted to cash. This is revealed by the accounts receivable turnover ratio, which is determined by dividing total revenue by the average accounts receivable. A refinement of this ratio uses only charge sales in the numerator; however, quite often charge sales figures are unavailable. Regardless of whether total revenue or charge sales are used as the numerator, the calculation should be consistent from period to period and from subject to benchmark.

To calculate the accounts receivable turnover, it is first necessary to determine the average accounts receivable. This is accomplished by adding accounts receivable at the beginning and end of the period and then dividing that figure by two. Once this is done, the accounts receivable turnover is calculated as follows:

$$\text{Accounts Receivable Turnover} = \frac{\text{Total Revenue}}{\text{Average Accounts Receivable}}$$

If *Any Spa* has accounts receivable balances as of May 31, X1 and X2, of $125,000 and $150,000 respectively, its average accounts receivable is $137,500. If total revenue is $3,000,000, *Any Spa's* accounts receivable turnover is $3,000,000 ÷ $137,500, or 21.8. This means that *Any Spa's* average accounts receivable is turned over 21.8 times per year.

Average Collection Period

This ratio reveals the number of days required to collect the average accounts receivable. The average collection period is calculated as follows:

$$\text{Average Collection Period} = \frac{\text{Days in Year}}{\text{Accounts Receivable Turnover}}$$

Given *Any Spa's* accounts receivable turnover of 21.8, it has an average collection period of 365 ÷ 21.8, or 16.7 days.

Solvency Ratios

Solvency ratios measure the degree to which a facility uses debt financing. These ratios reflect the ability of the spa to meet its long-term (more than one year) obligations. Owners view solvency ratios as a measure of their leverage and often prefer relatively low solvency ratios because low ratios indicate that debt is being used in place of equity to increase the return on the equity already invested. Creditors, on the other hand, prefer relatively high solvency ratios because high ratios reveal an equity cushion available to absorb any operating losses. Management is again caught in the middle, trying to satisfy owners by financing assets so as to maximize return on investments, and trying to satisfy creditors by not unduly jeopardizing the property's ability to meet its long-term obligations.

Solvency Ratio

A spa operation is solvent when its assets are greater than its liabilities. The solvency ratio compares total assets to total liabilities and is calculated as follows:

$$\text{Solvency Ratio} = \frac{\text{Total Assets}}{\text{Total Liabilities}}$$

If *Any Spa* has total assets of $3,750,000 and total liabilities of $750,000, its solvency ratio is $3,750,000 ÷ $750,000, or 5 to 1. This ratio reveals that for every $1 of liabilities, there are $5 in assets to pay those liabilities.

Debt-Equity Ratio

One of the most common solvency ratios is the debt-equity ratio, which compares the total liabilities of the operation to the total owners' equity in the operation and is calculated as follows:

$$\text{Debt-Equity Ratio} = \frac{\text{Total Liabilities}}{\text{Total Owners' Equity}}$$

If *Any Spa's* total owners' equity is $3,000,000 and its total liabilities are $750,000, its debt-equity ratio is $750,000 ÷ $3,000,000, or 25 percent. This ratio reveals the amount owed to creditors ($.25) for every $1 of owners' equity.

Activity Ratios

It is management's responsibility to generate earnings for owners while providing services and products to guests. Activity ratios measure the effectiveness with which management uses the spa's resources.

Inventory Turnover

This ratio measures the number of times inventory turns over during the period. Generally, owners prefer higher inventory turnover rates because high rates indicate that owners are not tying up excessive assets in inventory. To calculate inventory turnover, it is first necessary to determine the average inventory. This is accomplished by adding inventory at the beginning and end of the period and then dividing that figure by two. As an example of an inventory turnover ratio, consider the retail inventory turnover ratio, which is calculated as follows:

$$\text{Retail Inventory Turnover} = \frac{\text{Cost of Goods Sold}}{\text{Average Retail Inventory}}$$

If *Any Spa* has retail inventory balances as of May 31, X1 and X2, of $40,000 and $20,000 respectively, its average retail inventory is $30,000. If its cost of goods sold is $150,000, its retail inventory turnover is $150,000 ÷ $30,000, or 5 times per year.

Departmental Utilization by Treatment Room and/or Type

This ratio is essential in measuring management's ability to utilize available resources. To calculate this ratio the maximum number of treatments that can be performed per room and the actual number of treatments performed must be known.

$$\text{Departmental Utilization Rate} = \frac{\text{Number of Treatments Performed}}{\text{Maximum Number of Treatments that Can Be Performed}}$$

Assume that *Any Spa* is open 60 hours, or 3600 minutes, per week; that the average massage takes 90 minutes; and that there are two massage rooms, making a total of 7200 available minutes. The maximum number of treatments that can be performed equals 7200 minutes ÷ 90 minutes per treatment, or 80 treatments. If *Any Spa* performs 61 treatments in a given week, its utilization rate is 61 ÷ 80, or 76.3 percent. *Any Spa* is using its massage rooms 76.3 percent of the time.

Gross Margin Percentage

This ratio measures the gross margin percentage for treatment rooms. Management can use this ratio as a tool to determine if services should be discontinued and/or prices should be adjusted. The ratio is calculated by subtracting treatment room direct costs from treatment room revenue and then dividing the difference by the treatment room revenue.

$$\text{Gross Margin} = \text{Treatment Room Revenue} - \text{Treatment Room Direct Cost}$$

$$\text{Gross Margin Percentage} = \frac{\text{Gross Margin}}{\text{Treatment Room Revenue}}$$

Assume that *Any Spa* wants to calculate the gross margin percentage for its hydrotherapy room; that the spa is open 60 hours per week with weekly revenue of the room at $3500; and that each hydrotherapy treatment sells for $50, lasts 30 minutes, and costs $30 per treatment. Based on the above information, 70 treatments were given ($3,500 revenue ÷ $50 per treatment) and total direct costs for the week are $2,100 (70 treatments × $30 cost per treatment). *Any Spa's* gross margin percentage is 40 percent (that is, the gross margin of $1,400 divided by the treatment room revenue of $3,500).

Profitability Ratios

Profitability ratios reflect the overall effectiveness of management in producing the bottom line figure that owners and creditors expect. Owners invest in order to increase their wealth through dividends and increases in the value of the facility. Dividends and values are highly dependent on the present and future profits generated by the operation.

Caution should be used when using profitability ratios for comparison across competitive sets or comparable spas. Several factors influence the relative profitability of one type of spa (e.g., day spa vs. resort spa) among different spa types.

Profit Margin Ratio

This ratio measures management's overall ability to produce profits by generating sales and controlling expenses. The profit margin ratio is calculated as follows:

$$\text{Profit Margin Ratio} = \frac{\text{Net Income}}{\text{Total Revenue}}$$

The net income figure represents income after all expense deductions controlled by management and expenses directly related to decisions made by the property's owners have been deducted from revenue. If *Any Spa* has net income of $300,000 and total revenue of $3,000,000, its profit margin is $300,000 ÷ $3,000,000, or 10 percent.

Return on Assets Ratio (ROA)

This profitability ratio compares the net income of the spa to the average total assets. In essence, the results reveal the earning power of the spa's assets. The ROA is calculated as follows:

$$\text{ROA} = \frac{\text{Net Income}}{\text{Average Total Assets}}$$

If *Any Spa* has net income of $300,000 and average total assets of $3,750,000, its ROA is $300,000 ÷ $3,750,000, or 8 percent.

Return on Equity Ratio (ROE)

A third profitability ratio considers the spa's net income and the owners' investment. This ratio reveals the return to the owner based on the amount of their investment. The ROE is determined as follows:

$$\text{ROE} = \frac{\text{Net Income}}{\text{Average Owners' Equity}}$$

If *Any Spa* has net income of $300,000 and average owners' equity of $3,000,000, its ROE is $300,000 ÷ $3,000,000, or 10 percent.

Income before Fixed Charges per Treatment Room

This ratio measures management's ability to produce profits by generating sales and controlling all departmental costs. This ratio is calculated as follows:

$$\text{Income before Fixed Charges per Treatment Room} = \frac{\text{Income before Fixed Charges}}{\text{Number of Treatment Rooms}}$$

If *Any Spa* has 14 treatment rooms and income before fixed charges of $400,000, its income per treatment room before fixed charges is $400,000 ÷ 14, or $28,571.

Operating Ratios

Operating ratios help owners and management analyze spa operations. These ratios relate expenses to revenue.

Retail Revenue Contribution to Overall Revenue

This ratio measures retail sales contribution to overall revenue. Management can use this ratio as a tool to determine if retail training and/or price adjustments are needed. This ratio is calculated as follows:

$$\text{Retail Revenue Contribution} = \frac{\text{Retail Revenue}}{\text{Total Revenue}}$$

If *Any Spa* has retail revenue of $25,000 and total revenue of $190,000, its total revenue from retail sales is $25,000 ÷ $190,000, or 13.2 percent. This ratio can also be calculated by department to determine which department is maximizing its retail sales and which departments require additional sales training.

Revenue per Square Foot

This ratio is a measure of management's overall ability to generate sales by effectively using the available space. The revenue per square foot ratio is calculated as follows:

$$\text{Revenue per Square Foot} = \frac{\text{Total Revenue}}{\text{Total Square Footage}}$$

If *Any Spa* has 10,000 square feet of space and total revenue of $3,000,000, its revenue per square foot is $3,000,000 ÷ 10,000, or $300.

This ratio can also be calculated as profit per square foot. If *Any Spa* has net income of $300,000, its profit per square foot is $30. Departmental profit per square foot may be used to identify underperforming departments or service providers. The above examples can also be modified to calculate service revenue or retail revenue by square footage.

Labor Cost Percentage by Service Revenue and Retail Revenue

This ratio reveals management's ability to control labor costs in direct relation to the services performed and/or retail sold. This ratio is ideal when analyzing the payroll structures of comparable spas and can be calculated in total or on a departmental basis. To more efficiently control operations, calculate and analyze labor cost percentages by department. The labor cost percentage can be calculated as follows:

$$\text{Total (or Service) Labor Cost Percentage} = \frac{\text{Total (or Service) Labor Expense}}{\text{Total (or Service) Revenue}}$$

If *Any Spa* has skin care revenue of $50,000 for January X1 and skin care labor expense of $23,000, its skin care service labor cost is $23,000 ÷ $50,000, or 46 percent.

$$\text{Retail Labor Cost Percentage} = \frac{\text{Retail Labor Expense}}{\text{Retail Revenue}}$$

If *Any Spa* has retail revenue of $20,000 and retail labor expense paid to technicians of $4,000, its retail labor cost is $4,000 ÷ $20,000, or 20 percent. This ratio means that for every $100 of retail sold, $20 goes directly to the technicians.

Labor Cost per Treatment Room

An alternative method to measure labor costs is by dollars per available treatment room or per departmental treatment room. For those departments whose labor requirements are significantly influenced by the number of treatment rooms occupied (e.g., skin care and massage), labor cost per departmental treatment room is one measure of labor efficiency. For those departments whose labor requirements are not significantly influenced by the number of treatment rooms occupied (e.g., front desk and accounting), then labor cost per available treatment room is simply another measure of labor efficiency. The labor cost percentage can be calculated as follows:

$$\text{Labor Cost per Treatment Room} = \frac{\text{Total Labor Cost}}{\text{Total Treatment Rooms}}$$

If *Any Spa* has total staff payroll of $300,000 and eight treatment rooms, its total labor cost per treatment room is $300,000 ÷ 8, or $37,500.

$$\text{Labor Cost per Departmental Treatment Room} = \frac{\text{Departmental Labor Cost}}{\text{Departmental Treatment Rooms}}$$

If *Any Spa* has massage payroll of $45,000 and three massage rooms, its massage department's labor cost per treatment room is $45,000 ÷ 3, or $15,000.

Retail Cost of Sales Percentage

This ratio measures the profitability of retail sales. Management can use this ratio as a tool to determine whether retail training and/or price adjustments are needed. This ratio is calculated as follows:

$$\text{Retail Cost of Sales Percentage} = \frac{\text{Cost of Goods Sold}}{\text{Retail Revenue}}$$

If *Any Spa* has retail revenue of $25,000 and a cost of goods sold of $10,000, its retail cost of sales is $10,000 ÷ $25,000, or 40 percent.

Cost of Professional Products and Supplies Percentage

This ratio measures the efficiency of product usage per treatment. Management can use this ratio to determine whether professional products are being used efficiently. Each treatment has an average cost of product per treatment that can aid in the day-to-day management of the direct cost of the treatment. The average cost is vital to tracking the profitability of a treatment before any other direct costs such as labor are allocated. This ratio is calculated as follows:

$$\begin{array}{c}\text{Cost of Professional Products} \\ \text{and Supplies Percentage}\end{array} = \frac{\text{Cost of Professional Products Used}}{\text{Service Revenue}}$$

If *Any Spa* has revenue in the skin care department of $52,000 and has expended $5,000 of professional products, its cost of professional products and supplies used is $5,000 ÷ $52,000, or 9.6 percent.

Assume that *Any Spa* wants to compare its product usage at the technician level to the vendor's stated average product cost per treatment benchmark; that its average price per skin care treatment is $125, meaning *Any Spa* has performed 416 treatments ($52,000 ÷ $125 per treatment); and that its average professional product cost per treatment is therefore $12.02 ($5,000 ÷ 416 treatments). If the vendor's stated average product cost per treatment is $10, *Any Spa's* management knows that the spa's technicians are excessively using $2.02 of product per treatment.

Note: It is extremely important to track key operating expenses such as professional products and supplies, laundry, linen, and guest supplies as a cost per treatment. Without this information, management will not be able to determine which expenditures are out of line and require further analysis for any given period.

Discounts and Coupons

Discounts and coupons are used heavily in the spa industry to stimulate service and retail sales. Without careful analysis and frequent review, discounts and coupons can skew profitability comparisons from period to period. The average retail discount ratio and the average service discount ratio provide managers and owners the opportunity to monitor how revenues are affected by discount and coupon promotions.

$$\text{Average Retail Discount} = \frac{\text{Retail Discounts Given}}{\text{Total Retail Revenue}}$$

If *Any Spa* has $1,400 in retail discounts and total retail revenue of $15,000 in January X1, the average retail discount is $1,400 ÷ $15,000, or 9.3 percent.

Assume that in January X2, *Any Spa* has $11,125 in retail discounts and total retail revenue of $17,420. Comparison of these two periods will show a significant difference in the amount of discounts given (63.9 percent versus 9.3 percent). After careful review, management may determine (for example) that $9,325 of the discounts given in January X2 are attributable to a free robe promotion. After accounting for the free robe promotion, management is then able to determine that retail discounts from January X1 and January X2 were in fact comparable. That is, *Any Spa's* average retail discount for January X2 excluding the robe promotion is $1,800 ÷ $17,420, or 10.3 percent.

The calculation of the average service discount is similar:

$$\text{Average Service Discount} = \frac{\text{Service Discounts Given}}{\text{Total Service Revenue}}$$

If in February X1, *Any Spa* has $4,000 in service discounts and $70,000 in service revenue with no promotional offers, its average service discount is $4,000 ÷ $70,000, or 5.7 percent.

Assume that in February X2, *Any Spa* has $29,000 in service and promotional discounts and $120,000 in service revenue with a 20 percent discount promotion offered on all services. Management determines that the promotion in February X2 effectively increased gross revenues by $50,000 over the previous year ($120,000 minus $70,000) and net revenues by $26,000 ($50,000 minus the promotional discount of $24,000; $24,000 is calculated by multiplying $120,000 by 20 percent).

Revenue per Occupied Resort Room

This ratio measures the average amount of spa and fitness revenue generated by resort guests. Management uses this tool to determine whether internal sales marketing for the fitness and spa facilities is meeting its goals. This ratio is calculated as follows:

$$\text{Revenue per Occupied Room} = \frac{\text{Total Spa Revenues}}{\text{Number of Occupied Resort Rooms}}$$

If *The Spa at Any Resort* has total service, retail, and fitness facility revenue of $175,000 and *Any Resort* has 1600 occupied rooms for the period, each occupied room at *Any Resort* is contributing $175,000 ÷ 1600, or an average of $109.37 to *The Spa at Any Resort*.

Resort Capture Rates

These ratios measure the percentage of resort guests purchasing spa services and those using only the spa and fitness facilities. Management uses this tool to determine whether guests are using spa services and whether additional measures are required to generate sales. This ratio is calculated in two segments.

$$\text{Resort Capture Rate} = \frac{\text{Spa Service Resort Clients} + \text{Fitness Facilities Resort Clients}}{\text{Total Number of Resort Guests}}$$

$$\text{Resort Service Capture Rate} = \frac{\text{Spa Service Resort Clients}}{\text{Total Number of Resort Guests}}$$

Assume that *Any Resort* wants to know how many of its guests are using spa services and fitness facilities; that *Any Resort* had a total of 528 guests for the week;

that *The Spa at Any Resort* provided spa services to 115 guests, of whom 15 were walk-in guests not staying at the resort; and that an additional 247 resort guests used the fitness facilities. This means that approximately 65 percent of resort guests used the spa and fitness facilities (347 ÷ 528) and that 19 percent of resort guests purchased spa services (100 ÷ 528).

Resort Market Segmentation Capture Rate

Management uses this ratio to determine which market segments (i.e., group, transient, or local) are using spa services and facilities. Once this information is known, management can adjust marketing strategies to generate additional sales to the market segment they want to increase. Assume that *Any Resort* wants to know how the resort guests using spa services breaks down by market segment; that of *Any Resort's* 528 guests for the week, there were 316 group guests and 212 transient guests; and that *The Spa at Any Resort* saw 70 group guests, 30 transient guests, and 15 non-resort spa guests. This means that the capture rates are approximately 22 percent of the resort's group guests (70 ÷ 316) and 14 percent of the resort's transient guests (30 ÷ 212). Thirteen percent (15 ÷ 115) of spa guests were local guests not staying at the resort.

Other Important Operating Ratios

Management can use a number of other operating ratios for daily, monthly, or yearly comparative purposes. These other ratios include the following:

- *Average Service Revenue per Guest.* If *Any Spa* has $7,000 of service revenue and sees 47 guests on Thursday, its average service revenue per guest is $7,000 ÷ 47, or $148.94.

- *Average Retail Revenue per Guest.* If *Any Spa* has $1,500 of retail revenue on Thursday, its average retail revenue per guest is $1,500 ÷ 47, or $31.91.

- *Average Revenue per Employee.* If *Any Spa* has total revenue of $8,500 on Thursday and seven technicians, its average revenue per employee is $8,500 ÷ 7, or $1,214.86.

- *Average Dollar per Transaction.* If *Any Spa* has a total of 53 transactions on Thursday, its average dollar amount per transaction is $8,500 ÷ 53, or $160.38.

Section 10
Breakeven Analysis

The breakeven point of a spa operation is the level of revenue at which the facility's total revenue equals total costs. Although most operations desire to do much better than just break even financially, breakeven analysis serves as a reference point for managers planning operations for the period. The breakeven point can be illustrated by the following graph:

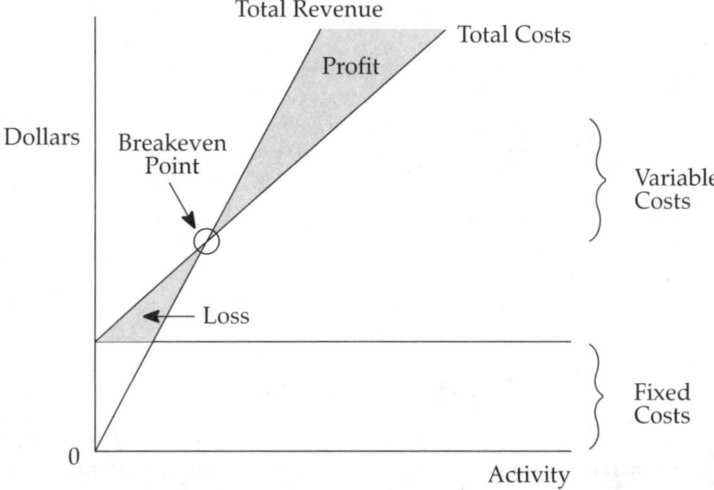

The graph shows that profit (net income) is zero at the breakeven point. The difference between the total revenue and total cost lines to the right of the breakeven point represents profit. The difference between the total revenue and total cost lines to the left of the breakeven point represents loss. A formula for determining the breakeven point is as follows:

$$\text{Breakeven Point} = \frac{\text{Fixed Costs}}{\text{Contribution Margin Percentage}}$$

To calculate the breakeven point, it is first necessary to determine fixed costs and the contribution margin percentage.

Fixed, Variable, and Mixed Costs

Spa operations incur three basic kinds of costs: fixed, variable, and mixed. Fixed costs are costs that remain constant in the short run, even though sales volume varies. Common examples of fixed costs include salaries, rent expense, insurance expense, property taxes, depreciation expense, and interest expense. Variable costs are costs that change proportionately with the volume of sales activity. For example, if the number of spa treatments increases by ten percent, the cost of related supplies for those treatments is expected to increase by ten percent. Mixed costs are costs composed of fixed and variable elements. An example of a mixed cost is telephone expense. Telephone expense is mixed because, although the basic cost of the system is fixed, variable costs arise in terms of usage rates that coincide with increases or decreases in activity.

In order to calculate the breakeven point, mixed costs must be divided into their fixed and variable elements. The high/low two-point method will be used to illustrate this division. Assume that a day spa during its busiest month (HM) provides 2,000 treatments and telephone expense is $400, while during the slowest month (LM) it provides 1,000 treatments and the telephone expense equals $300. The following formula is used to determine the estimated variable cost of telephone expense per treatment.

$$\frac{\text{Cost}_{\text{HM}} - \text{Cost}_{\text{LM}}}{\text{Treatments}_{\text{HM}} - \text{Treatments}_{\text{LM}}} = \text{variable cost per treatment}$$

$$\frac{\$400 - \$300}{2{,}000 - 1{,}000} = \frac{\$100}{1{,}000} = \$\underline{\underline{.10}} \text{ per treatment}$$

Then the fixed cost of the monthly telephone expense is determined as follows:

$$\begin{aligned} \text{Monthly fixed costs} &= \text{Total cost}_{\text{HM}} - \text{Variable cost}_{\text{HM}} \\ &= \$400 - \$.10(2{,}000) \\ &= \$200 \end{aligned}$$

Contribution Margin Percentage

The contribution margin percentage is the percentage of each sales dollar that is available to cover fixed costs. A formula for determining the contribution margin percentage follows:

$$\text{Contribution Margin Percentage} = \frac{\text{Total Revenue} - \text{Variable Costs}}{\text{Total Revenue}}$$

As an example, consider the Simplified Income Statement of the Sample Spa shown on the next page. To simplify the illustration, assume that all operated department expenses are variable costs and that all undistributed operating expenses are fixed costs.

The first step is to calculate the contribution margin percentage. To accomplish this, subtract the variable costs (the expenses of the operated departments in this example) from total revenue and then divide that figure by total revenue:

$$\text{Contribution Margin Percentage} = \frac{\$260{,}000 - \$139{,}000}{\$260{,}000} = \frac{\$121{,}000}{\$260{,}000} = \underline{\underline{46.54\%}}$$

This figure reveals that, after covering variable costs, 46.54% of each revenue dollar is available to cover fixed costs.

The second step is to calculate the breakeven point by dividing fixed costs by the contribution margin percentage. Since for the purposes of our illustration the fixed costs include the sum of the undistributed operating expenses, the breakeven point can be calculated as follows:

$$\text{Breakeven Point} = \frac{\$87{,}000}{.4654} = \underline{\underline{\$186{,}935.97}}$$

This figure reveals that the spa operation in this example needs $186,935.97 in total revenue in order to break even. Income taxes are ignored because at the breakeven point they are assumed to be zero. Revenues required to achieve various profit levels can be determined using modifications of breakeven analysis.

Sample Spa
Simplified Income Statement

	Revenue	Variable Expenses	Income (Loss)
OPERATED DEPARTMENTS			
Massage & Bodywork Services	$ 100,000	$ 50,000	$ 50,000
Skin Care Services	40,000	25,000	15,000
Hair Salon Services	55,000	30,000	25,000
Nail Salon Services	25,000	14,000	11,000
Retail	40,000	20,000	20,000
	$ 260,000	$ 139,000	$ 121,000
UNDISTRIBUTED OPERATING EXPENSES			
Support Labor			18,000
Indirect Operating Expenses			8,000
Operating Expenses—Facility			26,000
Administrative Expenses			22,000
Marketing Expenses			13,000
Total Undistributed Operating Expenses			87,000
NET OPERATING INCOME			34,000
INCOME TAXES			8,000
NET INCOME			$ 26,000

Section 11
Budgeting and Budgetary Controls

The process of creating an operating budget requires spa owners and managers to plan for the financial results they expect or desire over the coming budget period, typically one year. Once created, the operating budget itself serves owners and managers as a measure of how well the spa is achieving its goals during the budget period and, when needed, as a prompt for timely action to achieve a result. Performance to budget should be reviewed frequently. Annual operating budgets should be broken down by month and compared with actual results each month. Along with performance to budget, management should also compare the spa's performance with key indicator benchmarks. Variances from the budget or from key benchmarks may indicate the need to identify and analyze the cause of the variances. Understanding why a variance is occurring affords management the opportunity to take necessary corrective action. This section addresses the process of preparing, approving, implementing, and reviewing a budget.

Preparing the Budget

Budget preparation requires a substantial commitment from all levels of the organization. Budgeting is not merely an accounting department exercise. It requires participation and acceptance by departmental and senior managers.

The budgeting process begins with the immediate past. Historical financial information serves as a starting point for what is forecasted for the next period. In the absence of historical data, the budget process will more resemble the creation of a business plan and will be based on local industry averages.

There are two ways to begin the process: top down and bottom up. In the top-down process, management sets a gross revenue goal. Management may also set benchmarks in specific expense categories. For example, management may instruct that the spa hold its supply costs to a certain percentage of gross revenue. The leader of each division or business unit will then fill in the fixed and variable costs associated with achievement of the revenue goal.

The bottom-up method is reversed in that management sets a net income goal (the bottom line of the income statement). Departmental or divisional managers are then asked to prepare a budget that has sufficient revenue and related expenses to achieve the net income goal.

In either case, it is important that line managers (i.e., those responsible for performance) and senior managers agree not only on top line goals, but also on net operating profit percentages and achievability. The complete participation of the line managers is critical to producing a realistic budget. Goals that line managers do not perceive as reasonable are unlikely to be achieved. Having line managers participate in all aspects of the process can avoid this perception.

The accounting department should provide information to the operating departments along with a budget form that is consistent with the financial statements and schedules the spa uses to report its performance. Since service revenue is driven by the personal productivity of the service staff, it is key to anticipate hiring needs and employee turnover rates. Since the major cost is labor, manning schedules are an integral part of the budgeting process. For example, if management wants to increase gross revenues by 20 percent, it must ensure that it has the employees available to perform the services.

Timing is key and adherence to a schedule is essential. The spa should have a completed and approved budget at least one or two months before the start of the new period. The budget process should be completed in connection with the annual strategic planning for the spa. A suggested schedule for a spa on a calendar year schedule is as follows:

- *Four months prior to fiscal year end:* Schedule budget planning meetings and include all participants in the process. Prepare and hand out budget planning folders that include historical and industry financial and statistical data. Discussions should include overall budgeting goals, information needed to create the budget, and establishment of deadlines.
- *Three months before fiscal year end:* Department heads prepare critical issues, strategic objectives, and goals for the coming year. Out of this work should come the overall assumptions and revenue goals of the spa. These assumptions are then presented to the general manager/spa director for discussion and approval.
- *Two months prior to fiscal year end:* Department heads and the controller prepare budget plans based on agreed-upon objectives. These will include all operating and payroll expenses. Accounting personnel consolidate the departmental budgets into an overall master budget plan. These budgets are submitted to the general manager for approval.
- *One month prior to fiscal year end:* Strategic objectives should be revised in accordance with the updated budget plan, and final budget approval should be obtained.

Analyzing Objectives and Strategic Initiatives

Changes in business conditions, new initiatives at the spa, and personnel additions and deletions can all affect the budget. By reviewing the critical issues and strategic objectives, department heads can anticipate expenditures and revenues that may occur in the coming year. Combining this new information with historical data regarding continuing operations will provide the most accurate picture going forward.

Creating a Budget

The first step in the budget process is the review of historical results, market conditions, and conditions specific to the spa. Using the assumptions developed in the first stage of the process, the spa will create a top line budget by department.

Top-line budgeting for spas should be based on the number of customer visits and the average ticket. A ticket is defined as a customer transaction, which may include services, products, or both. The simplest way to arrive at a top-line sales budget starts with a projection of the number of customer visits anticipated for the period. (Resort spas often do this using a capture rate—for example, 12 percent of group guests.) If the budget for a spa that had 20,000 transactions in the previous year calls for an increase of 20 percent, this would mean a projection of 24,000 transactions for the next year. Industry data from similarly situated spas may be useful in determining an estimate of the quantity and types of customer transactions.

Based on historical or industry data, management can determine an estimated average sales per ticket. Management may choose to separate the service and retail elements of the average ticket. The anticipated service or retail revenue can then be calculated by multiplying the number of anticipated transactions by the average service sales or average retail sales per ticket.

Once the top line drivers are set, the next step is to calculate the associated direct variable costs. Service provider compensation (payroll cost) should be included in this calculation. For example, a spa that pays a 45 percent commission to massage therapists also adds about 3.44 percent (that is, 7.65 percent of that 45 percent) for payroll taxes for a total direct labor cost of 48.44 percent. Variable employee benefits should also be included in the payroll cost. Add to the total direct labor the cost of professional products used with provision of the service. This total is the direct variable cost percentage. Multiply the direct variable cost percentage by service sales to produce a budgeted cost. For example, if the average service ticket for a spa is $100, and the service providers are paid a 45 percent commission with an additional variable payroll cost and product cost of 15 percent, the cost of service would be 60 percent. Subtraction of direct variable cost from service revenue leaves a 40 percent service gross margin.

Other revenue sources include retail products and other goods sold to customers, including food and beverage, fitness activities, and health and wellness consultations. Retail, like service, can typically be forecasted by transaction. Historical data can provide the average retail sales per ticket. Retail revenue is then forecasted by multiplying the average retail sales per ticket by the expected number of transactions. The retail gross margin is calculated by subtracting the cost of goods from the retail sales. Activities and fitness revenue can be forecasted based on the price of those items multiplied by estimated guest utilization.

The total of the service and retail gross margin is total gross margin.

While not included in revenue until redeemed, gift certificate sales should also be forecasted for cash flow purposes. Gift certificate revenue is highly seasonal and contingent upon promotional activities and holidays.

Other Departmental Costs

After gross margin has been projected, other departmental costs associated with the delivery of a given service should be estimated. These include support labor (i.e., spa attendants) as well as other indirect expenses and overhead costs. These costs may be fixed or variable. For example, ambience costs such as candles will be fixed, while linen costs will vary by the treatment.

Unallocated Costs

Some of the operating costs associated with the day-to-day operations of the salon or spa are typically referred to as unallocated costs. These costs include, but are not limited to, advertising, promotions, printing, rent, janitorial service, repairs, maintenance, and management expense. Once again, historical financial data and strategic plans will provide a solid basis for estimating future expenses. The fixed costs are deducted from gross margin to compute a budgeted operating income or loss.

Review and Approval of General Managers Budget Report

An important exercise in the budget verification process is to compute each line item as a percentage of net sales (gross revenue less discounts) and to compare these percentages to the previous year's percentages. Any significant variance in the percentage could indicate an inadequate or overstated budget line. If not adjusted, significant variances should be justified in written budget notes.

In addition, projected cash flow is the definitive measure of a proposed budget's ability to provide for future operations and growth. In other words, will the proposed budget increase the cash balance at the end of 12 months? Remember, budgets are strategic planning tools for both short-term objectives and long-term growth. To prepare a simple projected cash flow, deduct any non-cash expenses, such as depreciation and amortization, and add back anticipated unredeemed gift certificate sales. Refer to Section 4 for a discussion of cash flow.

Once the senior management and departmental managers reach consensus on the goals and parameters set, the budget is ready for implementation. This budget, along with the critical issues identified in the beginning of the budget process, define the strategic initiatives of the spa for the coming year.

Implementation and Review of Budgets

It is essential to establish budgetary controls to achieve profit objectives. A monthly review of the budget identifies variances between budgeted amounts and the actual results of operations. Management should investigate and analyze significant variances to determine their exact causes. Discovery of the causes allows management to formulate a plan for corrective action.

Budget reports may be prepared on a monthly or quarterly basis. They should be prepared immediately following the close of the relevant period to help ensure that information on variances is discovered in time to take prompt corrective action. Department heads should be held accountable only for those budget items that are within their control. They should not be held accountable for allocated items such as interest, rent, or undistributed overhead, which are beyond their control. These items are the responsibility of senior management.

Certain non-income statement items should also be included in the budgetary review. For example, inventory management and purchasing protocols are essential for effective control. Periodic inventory counts (monthly, if possible) should be performed not only to determine actual amounts on hand, but also to identify possible waste and theft. Retail shelves should display enough inventory to provide the proper visual effect to consumers, and storage areas should contain only the amount of inventory necessary to meet customer demand. Purchase order protocols prevent unnecessary and unauthorized spending. Appointing a purchasing manager to monitor inventory and the types and quantities of goods purchased and to serve as a liaison with vendors provides controlled spending. Budgetary controls provide an environment for achievement of financial goals. Managers should be held accountable for balance sheet items that are under their direct control. Inventory is a good example of such an item, as it is the local manager who typically performs the inventory ordering.

Budget Summary and Key Indicators Report

Monthly financial statements that are measured against the budget are necessary to monitor success. A cover sheet summarizing results and significant variances should be attached to the financial statements. This budget summary should include a highlight of revenues, staffing and payroll costs, gross margin, total operating expenses, and net profit or loss. These should be compared with criteria set by the management team. Comments on significant issues that influence results should be written on the cover sheet. Coupled with the budget summary, a key indicators report should accompany the financial packet. Key indicators are statistical data based on actual results that are compared against benchmarks, which are discussed in Section 9 on ratio analysis. For instance, service payroll to service revenue is a key indicator for spas. Another example would be average number of clients per technician per week.

The budget summary, key indicators, and financial statements should be reviewed and discussed monthly in a scheduled financial review meeting. The parties who assisted in the budget preparation should be present in evaluating the outcome. The budget meeting is an excellent forum to discuss challenges and propose new ideas. New initiatives and operational directives often result from these discussions. Documentation and follow-through are essential to implementing these new ideas. The spa should share key results with the entire staff at periodic meetings to engage the whole team in the spa's financial performance.

Reforecasting

There are times when reforecasting or budget revisions are necessary due to significant variances from the initial plan. Typically, this is a result of swift economic changes or an altering of strategic plans. More often than not, revenues must be reforecasted and line item revisions are necessary, as opposed to a complete overhaul of the budget.

Part III
Financial Tools

Section 12
Sample Chart of Accounts

The following pages present a sample chart of accounts that is intended only as a guide to establishing an accounting system for recording business transactions. It is designed to be broad enough to have a major number for each account that is regularly used in standard reporting, and sufficiently detailed to provide sub-accounts for all departments or areas of significance.

The sample chart of accounts uses a ten-digit numbering system, consisting of three clusters: two clusters of three digits and one cluster of four digits. The clusters are broadly defined as follows:

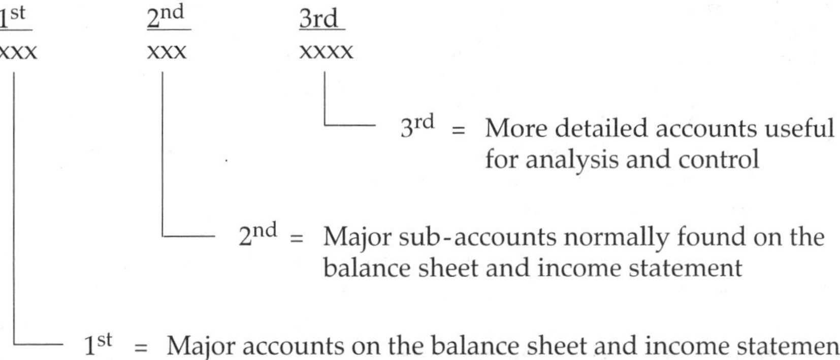

No attempt has been made to meet the specific needs of every spa operation. The chart of accounts presented here is sufficiently flexible to allow companies, individual owners, or managers to add or delete accounts to meet the needs and requirements of their spa operation. For example, a spa operation within a large resort environment that has limited reporting needs may choose to use only the first two clusters and a very selective reduced number of categories provided in the third cluster. Conversely, a very large day spa operation that requires a substantial amount of detail can add lines to the account numbering in the third cluster.

The following is provided as a guideline that will satisfy the information needed for the standardized reports and schedules. It also can be used to produce additional report information that may be valuable from an operational perspective.

The suggestions for assigning the digits within the first cluster identify the major primary categories found on the balance sheet and income statement as follows:

100 = Assets
150 = Liabilities
200 = Equity
250 = Revenue
300 = Allowances
350 = Cost of Goods Sold
400 = Direct Labor
450 = Other Direct Expenses
500 = Indirect Expenses
550 = Undistributed Operating Expenses
600 = Fixed Charges
650 = Federal and State Income Taxes

The digits within the second cluster in this sample chart identify the key subcategories that would fall under the major categories identified by the first cluster. For example, the first cluster number 100 identifies the major category "Assets" and, in the sample, you will see that the second cluster numbers identify the most common subcategories of assets as follows:

100 = Assets (Major category—first cluster)
- 100 = Current Assets (Sub category—second cluster)
- 200 = Non-current Receivables
- 300 = Non-current Investments
- 400 = Property and Equipment
- 500 = Other Non-current Assets

The suggested digit assignments within the third cluster identify the more detailed information that would fall under each subcategory identified by the second cluster. For example, following the primary category number 100, the second cluster number 100 identifies the major category "Assets" and, in the sample, you will see that the third cluster numbers identify the most common subcategories of assets.

The suggested digit assignments within the third cluster have two intents. First, all account numbers in this cluster that end in zero lend themselves to further expansion or "drilling down." Several examples of this can be seen in the sample chart of accounts that follows. As one example, one company might simply define Hair Product Inventories as account number 4020 within the fourth cluster, while another company might require more detail to identify the individual groups of hair products. In such a case, they could add accounts like 4021, 4023 and 4025 (as shown in the following pages), bearing in mind that all these accounts whose first three numbers are 402 can be consolidated or "rolled up" into the primary account 4020 for summarized reporting purposes.

The most important thing to keep in mind when refining the following chart of accounts to suit the needs of your spa operation is the data groupings that will be required to satisfy the standardized accounts and schedules in either long form or short form.

CHART OF ACCOUNTS

Account Number			Account Descriptions and Classifications	Related Schedules
			Assets—Current Assets	
100	**100**	**1000**	**Cash and Equivalents**	
		1010	**House Funds**	Balance Sheet
		1020	**Checking Account**	Balance Sheet
		1030	**Payroll Account**	Balance Sheet
		1040	**Savings Account**	Balance Sheet
		1050	**Petty Cash**	Balance Sheet
		2000	**Short-term Investments**	Balance Sheet
		3000	**Accounts Receivable**	Balance Sheet
		3010	**Guest Accounts**	Balance Sheet
		3020	**Credit Card Accounts**	Balance Sheet
		3030	**Notes Receivable (Current)**	Balance Sheet
		3040	**Current Maturities of Non-current Receivables**	Balance Sheet
		3050	**Due from Employees**	Balance Sheet
		3060	**Due from Owner**	Balance Sheet
		3070	**Other Accounts Receivable**	Balance Sheet
		3080	**Inter-company Receivables**	Balance Sheet
		3090	**Allowance for Doubtful Accounts**	Balance Sheet
		4000	**Inventories**	Balance Sheet
		4010	**Fitness—Inventories**	Balance Sheet
		4020	**Hair—Inventories**	Balance Sheet
		4021	Professional Color and Chemical Products	Balance Sheet
		4023	Professional Styling Products	Balance Sheet
		4025	Other Professional Products	Balance Sheet
		4030	**Health and Wellness—Inventories**	Balance Sheet
		4031	Professional Medical Products—Botox	Balance Sheet
		4033	Professional Medical Products—Chemicals for Peels	Balance Sheet
		4035	Professional Medical Products—Microdermabrasion	Balance Sheet
		4037	Professional Medical Products—Tissue Fillers and Supplies	Balance Sheet
		4039	Other Professional Products	Balance Sheet
		4040	**Massage—Inventories**	Balance Sheet
		4041	Professional Body Treatment Products	Balance Sheet
		4043	Professional Massage Treatment Products	Balance Sheet

		4035	Other Professional Products	Balance Sheet
		4050	**Nail—Inventories**	Balance Sheet
		4051	Professional Foot Care Products	Balance Sheet
		4053	Professional Hand Care Products	Balance Sheet
		4055	Other Professional Products	Balance Sheet
		4060	**Skin Care—Inventories**	Balance Sheet
		4061	Professional Body Treatment Products	Balance Sheet
		4063	Professional Facial Treatment Products	Balance Sheet
		4065	Professional Hair Removal Products	Balance Sheet
		4067	Other Professional Products	Balance Sheet
		4070	**Food and Beverage Inventories**	Balance Sheet
		4071	Beverage	Balance Sheet
		4073	Food	Balance Sheet
		4075	China, Glassware, Silver and Linen	Balance Sheet
		4077	Inventoried Operating Supplies	Balance Sheet
		4079	Other Inventory Items	Balance Sheet
		4080	**Retail Apparel Inventories**	Balance Sheet
		4081	Footwear	Balance Sheet
		4083	Retail Men's/Unisex Apparel	Balance Sheet
		4085	Robes	Balance Sheet
		4087	Women's Apparel	Balance Sheet
		4089	Retail Apparel	Balance Sheet
		4090	**Retail Book and Media Inventories**	Balance Sheet
		4100	**Retail Gifts and Accessories Inventories**	Balance Sheet
		4101	Retail Fashion Accessories	Balance Sheet
		4103	Retail Home Gifts and Accessories	Balance Sheet
		4105	Other Retail Gifts and Accessories	Balance Sheet
		4110	**Retail Spa Product Inventories**	Balance Sheet
		4111	Retail Body/Bath Products	Balance Sheet
		4113	Retail Hair Products	Balance Sheet
		4115	Retail Make-up Products	Balance Sheet
		4116	Retail Nail Products	Balance Sheet
		4117	Retail Skin Care Products	Balance Sheet
		4119	Other Retail Spa Product	Balance Sheet
		4120	**Retail Snacks and Beverage Inventories**	Balance Sheet
		4130	**Other Retail Inventories**	Balance Sheet
		4131	Retail Sundries	Balance Sheet
		4133	Other/Miscellaneous Retail	Balance Sheet
		4140	**Retail Supplies Inventories**	Balance Sheet

		4141	Gift Wrap and Packaging	Balance Sheet
		4143	Other Retail Supplies	Balance Sheet
		4150	**Operating Supplies Inventories**	Balance Sheet
		4151	Laundry Supplies	Balance Sheet
		4153	Linen and Terry	Balance Sheet
		4155	Uniforms	Balance Sheet
		4157	Other Inventoried Operating Supplies	Balance Sheet
		4160	**General and Administrative Office Supplies Inventory**	Balance Sheet
		4170	**Marketing Supplies and Collateral Materials Inventory**	Balance Sheet
		4180	**Repairs and Maintenance Inventory**	Balance Sheet
		4181	Cleaning Supplies	Balance Sheet
		4183	Pool Supplies	Balance Sheet
		4185	Other Facility Inventoried Items	Balance Sheet
		5000	**Prepaid Expenses**	Balance Sheet
		5010	Insurance	Balance Sheet
		5020	Taxes	Balance Sheet
		5030	Workers' Compensation	Balance Sheet
		5040	Supplies	Balance Sheet
		5050	Contracts	Balance Sheet
		5060	Current Deferred Tax Asset	Balance Sheet
		5070	Other Prepaid Expenses	Balance Sheet
		6000	**Other Current Assets**	Balance Sheet
			Assets—Non-current Receivables	
100	**200**	**1000**	**Non-current Receivables**	Balance Sheet
		1010	From Owners and Officers	Balance Sheet
		1030	Other Non-current Receivables	Balance Sheet
			Assets—Non-current Investments	
100	**300**	**1000**	**Non-current Investments**	Balance Sheet
			Assets—Property and Equipment	
100	**400**	**1000**	**Property and Equipment**	Balance Sheet
		1010	Land	Balance Sheet
		1020	Buildings	Balance Sheet
		1025	Accumulated Depreciation—Buildings	Balance Sheet
		1030	Leaseholds and Leasehold Improvements	Balance Sheet
		1035	Accumulated Depreciation—Leaseholds	Balance Sheet
		1040	Furniture and Fixtures	Balance Sheet
		1045	Accumulated Depreciation—Furniture and Fixtures	Balance Sheet
		1050	Machinery and Equipment	Balance Sheet

		1055	Accumulated Depreciation—Machinery and Equipment	Balance Sheet
		1060	Information Systems Equipment	Balance Sheet
		1065	Accumulated Depreciation—Information Systems Equipment	Balance Sheet
		1070	Automobiles and Trucks	Balance Sheet
		1075	Accumulated Depreciation—Automobiles and Trucks	Balance Sheet
		1080	Construction In Progress	Balance Sheet
		1090	China, Glassware, Silver, Linen, Uniforms	Balance Sheet
		1095	Accumulated Depreciation—China, Glassware, Silver, Linen, Uniforms	Balance Sheet
			Assets—Other Non-current Assets	
100	**500**	**1000**	**Other Assets**	Balance Sheet
		1010	Security and Lease Deposits	Balance Sheet
		1020	Loan Fees	Balance Sheet
		1030	Intangibles	Balance Sheet
		1040	Organizational Costs	Balance Sheet
		1050	Deferred Charges	Balance Sheet
		1060	Long-term Deferred Tax Asset	Balance Sheet
		1070	Other Non-current Assets	Balance Sheet
			Liabilities—Current Liabilities	
150	**100**	**1000**	**Current Payables**	Balance Sheet
		1010	Accounts Payable	Balance Sheet
		1020	Dividends Payable	Balance Sheet
		1030	Notes Payable	Balance Sheet
		1040	Inter-company Payables	Balance Sheet
		2000	**Employee Withholdings**	Balance Sheet
		2010	FICA—Employee	Balance Sheet
		2020	State Disability—Employee	Balance Sheet
		2030	SUTA—Employee	Balance Sheet
		2040	Medical Insurance—Employee	Balance Sheet
		2050	Life Insurance—Employee	Balance Sheet
		2060	Dental Insurance—Employee	Balance Sheet
		2070	Credit Union	Balance Sheet
		2080	United Way	Balance Sheet
		2090	Miscellaneous Employee Deductions	Balance Sheet
		3000	**Employer Payroll Taxes**	Balance Sheet
		3010	FICA—Employer	Balance Sheet
		3020	FUTA—Employer	Balance Sheet
		3030	SUTA—Employer	Balance Sheet
		3040	Medical Insurance—Employer	Balance Sheet

		3050	Life Insurance—Employer	Balance Sheet
		3060	Dental Insurance—Employer	Balance Sheet
		3070	Disability—Employer	Balance Sheet
		3080	Workers' Compensation—Employer	Balance Sheet
		3090	Miscellaneous Employer Contributions	Balance Sheet
		4000	**Taxes**	Balance Sheet
		4010	Federal Withholding Taxes	Balance Sheet
		4020	State Withholding Taxes	Balance Sheet
		4030	Country Withholding Taxes	Balance Sheet
		4040	City Withholding Taxes	Balance Sheet
		4050	Sales Tax	Balance Sheet
		4060	Property Tax	Balance Sheet
		4070	Federal Income Tax	Balance Sheet
		4080	State Income Tax	Balance Sheet
		4090	City Income Tax	Balance Sheet
		5000	**Advance Deposits**	Balance Sheet
		6000	**Accrued Expenses**	Balance Sheet
		6010	Accrued Payables	Balance Sheet
		6020	Accrued Utilities	Balance Sheet
		6030	Accrued Vacation	Balance Sheet
		6040	Accrued Taxes	Balance Sheet
		6050	Accrued Expenses—Other	Balance Sheet
		7000	**Current Portion of Long-term Debt**	Balance Sheet
		8000	**Deferrals**	Balance Sheet
		8010	Current Deferred Tax Liability	Balance Sheet
		8020	Deferred Revenue—Gift Certificates—Current Portion	Balance Sheet
		8030	Deferred Revenue—Other	Balance Sheet
		9000	**Other Current Liabilities**	Balance Sheet
			Liabilities—Long-term Debt Net of Current Maturities	
150	**200**	**1000**	**Long-term Debt Net of Current Maturities**	Balance Sheet
		1010	Long-term Notes and Other Similar Liabilities	Balance Sheet
		1020	Long-term Obligations Under Capital Leases	Balance Sheet
		1030	Long-term Debt—Owners and Officers	Balance Sheet
		2000	**Non-current Deferred Revenues**	Balance Sheet
		2010	Deferred Revenue—Gift Certificates—Non-current Portion	Balance Sheet
		2020	Other Deferred Revenue	Balance Sheet
		3000	**Non-current Deferred Income Taxes**	Balance Sheet
		4000	**Non-current Commitments and Contingencies**	Balance Sheet

Equity

			FOR CORPORATIONS	
200	**100**	**1000**	**Stockholders' Equity**	Balance Sheet
		1010	Capital stock	Balance Sheet
		1020	Additional Paid-in Capital	Balance Sheet
		1030	Retained Earnings	Balance Sheet
		1040	Treasury Stock	Balance Sheet
		1050	Unrealized Gain (Loss) on Marketable Equity Securities	Balance Sheet
		1060	Cumulative Foreign Currency Translation Adjustments	Balance Sheet
		1070	Income Summary	Balance Sheet
			FOR PARTNERSHIPS	
200	**100**	**1000**	**Partners' Equity**	Balance Sheet
		1010	General Partners' Capital Accounts	Balance Sheet
		1020	Limited Partners' Capital Accounts	Balance Sheet
		1030	General Partners' Withdrawals	Balance Sheet
		1040	Limited Partners' Withdrawals	Balance Sheet
		1050	Income Summary	Balance Sheet
			FOR LIMITED LIABILITY COMPANY	
200	**100**	**1000**	**Members' Equity**	Balance Sheet
		1010	Members' Capital Accounts	Balance Sheet
		1020	Members' Withdrawals	Balance Sheet
		1030	Income Summary	Balance Sheet
			FOR SOLE PROPRIETORSHIPS	
200	**100**	**1000**	**Owner's Equity**	Balance Sheet
		1010	Owner's Capital Accounts	Balance Sheet
		1020	Owner's Withdrawals	Balance Sheet
		1030	Income Summary	Balance Sheet

Revenue

250	**100**	**1000**	**Massage Revenue**	1
		1010	**Relaxation and Therapeutic**	1
		1020	**Specialty**	1
		1021	Thai Massage	1
		1023	Hot Stone Massage	1
		1025	Watsu	1
		1027	Other Specialty Massage	1
		1030	**Body Treatments**	1
		1040	**Hydrotherapy**	1
		1050	**Wraps and Scrubs**	1

	1051	Body Scrubs	1
	1053	Body Polishes	1
	1055	Salt Glows	1
	1060	**Specialty Body Treatments**	1
	1070	**Other Massage**	1
	1071	Breakage	1
	1073	Service Charges	1
	1075	Other	1
150	**1000**	**Skin Care Revenue**	2
	1020	**Facial Treatments**	2
	1021	Specialty	2
	1023	Standard	2
	1030	**Waxing Services**	2
	1031	Body	2
	1033	Bikini	2
	1035	Brazilian	2
	1037	Face	2
	1039	Back	2
	1040	**Other Skin Care**	2
	1041	Breakage	2
	1043	Consultations/Analysis	2
	1045	Service Charges	2
	1047	Other	2
200	**1000**	**Hair Revenue**	3
	1010	**Color and Chemical**	3
	1011	Color	3
	1013	Perms and Relaxers	3
	1020	**Styling**	3
	1021	Extensions	3
	1023	Haircuts	3
	1025	Specialty Styling	3
	1030	**Other Hair**	3
	1031	Breakage	3
	1033	Sevice Charges	3
	1035	Other	3
250	**1000**	**Nail Revenue**	4
	1010	**Manicure**	4
	1011	Nail Enhancements	4
	1013	Specialty	4

	1015	Standard		4
	1020	**Pedicure**		4
	1021	Specialty		4
	1023	Standard		4
	1030	**Other Nail**		4
	1031	Breakage		4
	1033	Service Charges		4
	1035	Other		4
300	**1000**	**Fitness Revenue**		5
	1010	**Personal Training**		5
	1031	Individual Coaching		5
	1033	Fitness Training		5
	1035	Fitness Program Development		5
	1037	Other Personal Training		5
	1020	**Group Exercise**		5
	1021	Aerobics		5
	1023	Pilates		5
	1025	Feldenkrais		5
	1027	Yoga		5
	1029	Other Fitness Classes		5
	1030	**Fitness Evaluations**		5
	1040	**Service Charges**		5
	1050	**Other Fitness**		5
350	**1000**	**Food and Beverage Revenue**		6
	1010	Beverage		6
	1020	Food		6
	1030	Other Food and Beverage		6
400	**1000**	**Health and Wellness Revenue**		7
	1010	**Medically Supervised Services**		7
	1011	Botox		7
	1012	Chemical Peels		7
	1013	Laser Hair Removal		7
	1014	Medical Esthetics Consultation		7
	1015	Medical Microdermabrasion		7
	1016	Nutritional Counseling		7
	1017	Photofacials/Intense Pulse Light		7
	1018	Soft Tissue Fillers—Collagen, Restylane, Perlane, etc.		7
	1019	Other Medical Spa Treatments		7
	1020	**Nutrition**		7

	1030	**Wellness Consultations**	7
	1033	Smoking Cessation	7
	1035	Weight Loss	7
	1037	Other Lifestyle Consultations	7
	1040	**Wellness Programs**	7
	1041	Smoking Cessation	7
	1043	Weight Loss	7
	1045	Other Lifestyle Workshops	7
	1050	**Breakage**	7
	1051	Charges for Unused Portions of Spa Packages or Series	7
	1053	No Show Charges	7
	1055	Cancellation Charges	7
	1057	Other Breakage Charges	7
	1060	**Service Charges**	7
	1070	**Other Health and Wellness**	7
450	**1000**	**Membership Revenue**	8
	1010	Daily Facility/Guest Fees	8
	1020	Initiation Fees	8
	1030	Membership Dues	8
	1040	Other Membership	8
500	**1000**	**Retail Revenue**	9
	1010	**Apparel**	9
	1011	Footwear	9
	1013	Men's/Unisex	9
	1015	Robes and Terry	9
	1017	Women's	9
	1020	**Gifts and Accessories**	9
	1021	Books and Media	9
	1023	Fashion Accessories	9
	1025	Home	9
	1030	**Products**	9
	1031	Bath and Body Products	9
	1032	Hair Products	9
	1033	Nail Products	9
	1035	Make-up Products	9
	1037	Private Label Products	9
	1039	Skin Care Products	9
	1040	**Other Retail**	9
	1041	Snacks and Beverages	9

		1043	Sundries	9
		1045	Other	9
	550	**1000**	**Other Operating Departments**	10
		1010	**Make-up Revenue**	10
		1011	Application	10
		1013	Specialty	10
		1015	Consultations	10
		1017	Other	10
		1020	**Other Revenue**	10
		1021	Misc. Consultative Services	10
		1023	Equestrian	10
		1025	Children's Programs and Daycare	10
		1037	Rock Climbing	10
		1039	Other	10
	600	**1000**	**Rental and Other Income**	11
		1010	Space Rentals and Concessions	11
		1020	Cash Discounts Earned	11
		1030	Cancellation and Unredeemed Gift Certificates	11
		1040	Foreign Currency Transactions Gains (Losses)	11
		1050	Interest Income	11
		1060	Other	11
			Allowances	
300	**100**	**1000**	**Allowances—Massage**	1
		1010	Service Allowances	1
		1020	Discounts Given	1
	200	**1000**	**Allowances—Skin Care**	2
		1010	Service Allowances	2
		1020	Discounts Given	2
	300	**1000**	**Allowances—Hair**	3
		1010	Service Allowances	3
		1020	Discounts Given	3
	400	**1000**	**Allowances—Nail**	4
		1010	Service Allowances	4
		1020	Discounts Given	4
	500	**1000**	**Allowances—Fitness**	5
		1010	Service Allowances	5
		1020	Discounts Given	5
		1000	**Allowances—Food and Beverage**	6
		1010	Service Allowances	6

		1020	Discounts Given	6
	600	**1000**	**Allowances—Health and Wellness**	7
		1010	**Service Allowances**	7
		1011	Medically Supervised Services	7
		1013	Other	7
		1020	**Discounts Given**	7
		1021	Medically Supervised Services	7
		1023	Other	7
	700	**1000**	**Allowances—Membership**	8
		1010	Initiation Fee Refunds	8
		1020	Other	8
	800	**1000**	**Revenue Adjustments—Retail**	9
		1010	Employee Discounts	9
		1020	Merchandise Returns	9
		1030	Allowances	9
	900	**1000**	**Allowances—Other Operating Departments**	10
		1010	Service Allowances	10
		1020	Discounts Given	10

Cost of Goods Sold

350	**100**	**1000**	**Cost of Goods Sold—Food and Beverage**	6
		1010	Food Costs	6
		1020	Beverage Costs	6
	200	**1000**	**Cost of Goods Sold—Retail**	9
		1010	**Apparel**	9
		1011	Footwear	9
		1013	Men's/Unisex	9
		1015	Robes and Terry	9
		1017	Women's	9
		1020	**Gifts and Accessories**	9
		1021	Books and Media	9
		1023	Fashion Accessories	9
		1025	Home	9
		1030	**Products**	9
		1031	Bath and Body Products	9
		1032	Hair Products	9
		1033	Nail Products	9
		1035	Make-up Products	9
		1037	Private Label Products	9
		1039	Skin Care Products	9

		1040	**Other Retail**	9
		1041	Snacks and Beverages	9
		1043	Sundries	9
		1045	Other	9
	300	**1000**	**Cost of Goods Sold—Other Operating Departments**	10

Direct Labor

400	**100**	**1000**	**Salaries and Wages**	
		1100	**Massage**	1
		1110	Massage	1
		1120	Body Treatments	1
		1130	Other	1
		1200	**Skin Care**	2
		1210	Facial Treatments	2
		1220	Waxing Services	2
		1230	Other	2
		1300	**Hair**	3
		1310	Color and Chemical	3
		1320	Styling	3
		1330	Other	3
		1400	**Nail**	4
		1410	Manicure	4
		1420	Pedicure	4
		1430	Other	4
		1500	**Fitness**	5
		1600	**Food and Beverage**	6
		1700	**Health and Wellness**	7
		1800	**Retail**	9
		1900	**Other Operating Departments**	10
	200	**100**	**Commissions**	
		1100	**Massage**	1
		1110	Massage	1
		1120	Body Treatments	1
		1130	Other	1
		1200	**Skin Care**	2
		1210	Facial Treatments	2
		1220	Waxing Services	2
		1230	Other	2
		1300	**Hair**	3
		1310	Color and Chemical	3

	1320	Styling	3
	1330	Other	3
	1400	**Nail**	4
	1410	Manicure	4
	1420	Pedicure	4
	1430	Other	4
	1500	**Fitness**	5
	1700	**Health and Wellness**	7
	1800	**Retail**	9
	1900	**Other Operating Departments**	10
300	**100**	**Contract**	
	1100	**Massage**	1
	1110	Massage	1
	1120	Body Treatments	1
	1130	Other	1
	1200	**Skin Care**	2
	1210	Facial Treatments	2
	1220	Waxing Services	2
	1230	Other	2
	1300	**Hair**	3
	1310	Color and Chemical	3
	1320	Styling	3
	1330	Other	3
	1400	**Nail**	4
	1410	Manicure	4
	1420	Pedicure	4
	1430	Other	4
	1500	**Fitness**	5
	1700	**Health and Wellness**	7
	1900	**Other Operating Departments**	10
400	**100**	**Distributed Service Charges**	
	1100	**Massage**	1
	1110	Massage	1
	1120	Body Treatments	1
	1130	Other	1
	1200	**Skin Care**	2
	1210	Facial Treatments	2
	1220	Waxing Services	2
	1230	Other	2

		1300	**Hair**	3
		1310	Color and Chemical	3
		1320	Styling	3
		1330	Other	3
		1400	**Nail**	4
		1410	Manicure	4
		1420	Pedicure	4
		1430	Other	4
		1500	**Fitness**	5
		1700	**Health and Wellness**	7
		1900	**Other Operating Departments**	10
	500	**1000**	**Payroll Taxes and Employee Benefits**	
		1100	**Massage**	1
		1110	**Massage**	1
		1111	Payroll Taxes	1
		1113	Insurance	1
		1114	Pension	1
		1115	Employee Meals	1
		1117	Vacation/Holiday	1
		1119	Other Taxes and Benefits	1
		1120	**Body Treatments**	1
		1121	Payroll Taxes	1
		1123	Insurance	1
		1124	Pension	1
		1125	Employee Meals	1
		1127	Vacation/Holiday	1
		1129	Other Taxes and Benefits	1
		1130	**Other**	1
		1131	Payroll Taxes	1
		1133	Insurance	1
		1134	Pension	1
		1135	Employee Meals	1
		1137	Vacation/Holiday	1
		1139	Other Taxes and Benefits	1
		1200	**Skin Care**	2
		1210	Facial Treatments	2
		1220	Waxing Services	2
		1230	Other	2
		1300	**Hair**	3

		1310	Color and Chemical	3
		1320	Styling	3
		1330	Other	3
		1400	**Nail**	4
		1410	Manicure	4
		1420	Pedicure	4
		1430	Other	4
		1500	**Fitness**	5
		1600	**Food and Beverage**	6
		1700	**Health and Wellness**	7
		1800	**Retail**	9
		1900	**Other Operating Departments**	10
			Other Direct Expenses	
450	**100**	**1000**	**Professional Products and Supplies Expense**	
		1100	**Massage**	1
		1110	Massage	1
		1120	Body Treatments	1
		1130	Other	1
		1200	**Skin Care**	2
		1210	Facial Treatments	2
		1220	Waxing Services	2
		1230	Other	2
		1300	**Hair**	3
		1310	Color and Chemical	3
		1320	Styling	3
		1330	Other	3
		1400	**Nail**	4
		1410	Manicure	4
		1420	Pedicure	4
		1430	Other	4
		1500	**Health and Wellness**	7
	200	**1000**	**Other Direct Fitness Expenses**	5
		1110	Ambience	5
		1111	Background Music	5
		1113	Candles	5
		1115	Aromatherapy Oils	5
		1117	Diffusers	5
		1119	Other Ambience Expenses	5
		1120	Athletic Supplies	5

		1221	Ropes for Fitness Classes	5
		1223	Racquet Ball and Tennis Supplies	5
		1225	Pool Items—Kick Boards etc.	5
		1227	Basketball and Volleyball Supplies	5
		1227	Other Athletic Equipment	5
		1130	Contract Services	5
		1140	Equipment Rentals	5
		1441	Fitness Equipment Rentals	5
		1445	Other Equipment Rental	5
		1150	Guest Supplies	5
		1151	Shampoo	5
		1153	Lotions	5
		1155	Razors and Shaving Creams	5
		1157	Other Locker Room Supplies	5
		1160	Hospitality	5
		1161	Bottled Water	5
		1163	Juice	5
		1165	Coffee and Tea	5
		1167	Cups, Utensils and Napkins	5
		1169	Other Hospitality Supplies	5
		1170	Laundry	5
		1171	Outside Laundry Services	5
		1173	In-house Laundry Supplies and Chemicals	5
		1175	Other Laundry Expenses	5
		1180	Licenses	5
		1183	Federal Operating Licenses	5
		1185	State Operating Licenses	5
		1187	Municipal Operating Licenses	5
		1188	Music Licenses	5
		1189	Other Licenses	5
		1190	Linen	5
		1191	Sheets	5
		1193	Towels	5
		1195	Treatment Room Pads	5
		1196	Treatment Room Blankets	5
		1197	Bath Mats	5
		1199	Other Linen	5
		1200	Operating Supplies	5
		1201	Cleaning Supplies	5

	1203	Printed Forms Used by Employees	5
	1205	Facial Tissue, Toilet Paper and Other Paper Supplies	5
	1207	Office Supplies Used in Operations	5
	1209	Other Operating Supplies Inventory	5
	1210	Professional Development	5
	1211	Training Materials	5
	1213	Training Supplies	5
	1215	3rd Party Instructor Fees	5
	1217	Outside Seminars and Courses	5
	1219	Other Professional Development Expenses	5
	1220	Telecommunications	5
	1221	Telephone Usage Charges	5
	1223	Telephone Equipment Charges	5
	1225	Cell Phone and Pager Charges	5
	1227	Internet and E-mail Charges	5
	1229	Other Telecommunications Expenses	5
	1230	Uniforms	5
	1231	Spa Employee Uniforms	5
	1233	Uniform Cleaning and Repair	5
	1235	Other Uniform Expenses	5
	1240	Other	5
300	**1000**	**Other Direct Food and Beverage Expenses**	6
	1110	Banquet and Party Costs	6
	1120	China, Glassware, Silver and Linen	6
	1130	Contract Services	6
	1140	Dues and Subscriptions	6
	1150	Equipment Rentals	6
	1160	Kitchen Utensils	6
	1170	Laundry	6
	1180	Licenses/Fees	6
	1190	Operating Supplies	6
	1200	Professional Development	6
	1210	Telecommunications	6
	1220	Uniforms	6
	1230	Other	6
400	**1000**	**Other Direct Retail Expenses**	9
	1110	Buying Trips	9
	1120	Contract Services	9
	1130	Equipment Rentals	9

		1140	Gift Wrap and Packaging	9
		1150	Licenses and Fees	9
		1160	Merchandise Displays and Accessories	9
		1170	Merchandise Tags	9
		1180	Operating Supplies	9
		1190	Packaging and Freight	9
		1200	Professional Development	9
		1210	Telecommunications	9
		1220	Uniforms	9
		1230	Other Retail Expenses	9
	500	**1000**	**Other Direct Other Operating Departments Expenses**	10
		1110	China, Glass and Linen	10
		1120	Contract Services	10
		1130	Equipment Rental	10
		1140	Guest Supplies	10
		1150	Laundry	10
		1160	Licenses	10
		1170	Operating Supplies	10
		1180	Professional Development	10
		1190	Telecommunications	10
		1200	Uniforms	10
		1210	Other	10

Indirect Expenses

500	**100**	**1000**	**Indirect Support Labor**	12
		1100	**Salaries and Wages**	12
		1110	Guest Reception	12
		1120	Host(ess)/Attendant	12
		1130	Housekeeping	12
		1140	Reservations	12
		1150	Supervision	12
		1160	Commissions	12
		1170	Distributed Service Charges	12
		1180	Payroll Taxes and Employee Benefits	12
		1181	Payroll Taxes	12
		1183	Insurance	12
		1184	Pension	12
		1185	Employee Meals	12
		1187	Vacation/Holiday	12
		1189	Other Taxes and Benefits	12

200	**1000**	**Indirect Operating Expenses**	13
	1010	Ambience	13
	1011	Background Music	13
	1013	Candles	13
	1015	Aromatherapy Oils	13
	1017	Diffusers	13
	1019	Other Ambience Expenses	13
	1020	Contract Services	13
	1021	Janitorial Services	13
	1023	Window Washing	13
	1025	Carpet Cleaning	13
	1027	Other Contract Services	13
	1030	Dues and Subscriptions	13
	1031	ISPA Membership and Fees	13
	1033	Chamber of Commerce	13
	1035	Newspapers and Magazines	13
	1037	Other Dues and Subscriptions	13
	1040	Equipment Rental	13
	1041	Spa Services Equipment Rentals	13
	1045	Other Equipment Rentals	13
	1050	Guest Clothing	13
	1051	Robes	13
	1053	Sandals	13
	1055	Smocks and Workout Attire	13
	1056	Wraps and Turbans	13
	1057	Disposable Swimwear	13
	1059	Other Guest Clothing	13
	1060	Guest Supplies	13
	1061	Locker Room Shampoo	13
	1063	Locker Room Soap	13
	1065	Locker Room Razors, Q-Tips, Shave Cream, Cotton Balls etc.	13
	1067	Hair Dryers, Combs and Brushes	13
	1069	Other Guest Supplies	13
	1070	Hospitality	13
	1071	Bottled Water	13
	1073	Juice	13
	1075	Coffee and Tea	13
	1077	Cups, Utensils and Napkins	13
	1079	Other Hospitality Supplies	13

		1080	Laundry	13
		1081	Outside Laundry Services	13
		1083	In-house Laundry Supplies and Chemicals	13
		1085	Other Laundry Expenses	13
		1090	Licenses and Fees	13
		1091	Federal Operating Licenses	13
		1093	State Operating Licenses	13
		1095	Municipal Operating Licenses	13
		1097	Music Licenses	13
		1099	Other Licenses and Fees	13
		1100	Linen	13
		1101	Sheets	13
		1103	Towels	13
		1105	Treatment Room Pads	13
		1106	Treatment Room Blankets	13
		1107	Bath Mats	13
		1109	Other Linen and Terry	13
		1110	Operating Supplies	13
		1111	Cleaning Supplies	13
		1113	Printed Forms Used by Employees	13
		1115	Facial Tissue, Toilet Paper and Other Paper Supplies	13
		1117	Office Supplies Used In Operations	13
		1119	Other Operating Supplies Inventory	13
		1120	Professional Development	13
		1121	Training Materials	13
		1123	Training Supplies	13
		1125	Third-party Instructor Fees	13
		1127	Outside Seminars and Courses	13
		1129	Other Professional Development Expenses	13
		1130	Telecommunications	13
		1131	Telephone Usage Charges	13
		1133	Telephone Equipment Charges	13
		1135	Cell Phone and Pager Charges	13
		1137	Internet and E-mail Charges	13
		1139	Other Telecommunications Expenses	13
		1140	Uniforms	13
		1141	Spa Employee Uniforms	13
		1143	Uniform Cleaning and Repair	13
		1145	Other Uniform Expenses	13
		1150	Other	13

			Undistributed Operating Expenses	
550	**100**	**1000**	**Administrative and General Expenses**	14
		1100	Payroll and Related Expenses	14
		1110	Salaries and Wages	14
		1111	Management Salaries	14
		1113	Administrative Salaries	14
		1120	Payroll Taxes and Employee Benefits	14
		1121	Payroll Taxes	14
		1123	Insurance	14
		1124	Pension	14
		1125	Employee Meals	14
		1127	Vacation/Holiday	14
		1129	Other Taxes and Benefits	14
		1200	Accounting Expenses	14
		1210	Audit and Other External Expenses	14
		1220	Payroll Processing Expenses	14
		1230	Other Accounting Expenses	14
		1300	Other	14
		1303	Bank Charges	14
		1306	Cash Over/Short	14
		1309	Contract Services	14
		1312	Corporate Office Charges	14
		1315	Credit and Collection	14
		1318	Credit Card Commission	14
		1321	Donations	14
		1324	Dues and Subscriptions	14
		1327	Human Resources	14
		1330	Information Systems	14
		1333	Legal and Professional	14
		1336	Licenses and Fees	14
		1339	Loss and Damage	14
		1342	Meals and Entertainment	14
		1345	Operating Supplies	14
		1348	Postage	14
		1351	Professional Development	14
		1354	Provision for Doubtful Accounts	14
		1357	Security	14
		1360	Telecommunications	14
		1363	Travel	14

	1366	Other	14
200	**1000**	**Marketing Expenses**	15
	1100	Salaries and Wages	15
	1200	Payroll Taxes and Employee Benefits	15
	1210	Payroll Taxes	15
	1220	Insurance	15
	1230	Pension	15
	1240	Employee Meals	15
	1250	Vacation/Holiday	15
	1260	Other Taxes and Benefits	15
	1300	Other	15
	1303	Advertising Broadcast	15
	1306	Advertising Print	15
	1309	Agency Fees	15
	1312	Complimentary Guests	15
	1315	Collateral Materials	15
	1318	Contract Services	15
	1321	Direct Mail	15
	1324	Dues and Subscriptions	15
	1327	In-house Promotions	15
	1330	Meals and Entertainment	15
	1333	Postage	15
	1336	Professional Development	15
	1339	Special Events	15
	1342	Trade Shows	15
	1345	Telecommunication	15
	1348	Travel	15
	1351	Other Marketing	15
300	**1000**	**Facility Maintenance Expenses**	16
	2000	Salaries and Wages	16
	3000	Payroll Taxes and Employee Benefits	16
	3010	Payroll Taxes	16
	3020	Insurance	16
	3030	Pension	16
	3040	Employee Meals	16
	3050	Vacation/Holiday	16
	3060	Other Taxes and Benefits	16
	4000	Facility Maintenance	16
	4010	Building	16

		4011	Interior Repairs and Maintenance	16
		4013	Exterior Repairs and Maintenance	16
		4015	Other Building Repairs and Maintenance	16
		4020	Contract Services	16
		4021	Elevator Maintenance	16
		4023	Inspection Contracts	16
		4025	Pest Control Contracts	16
		4027	Other Contract Services	16
		4030	Equipment Rentals	16
		4031	Maintenance Equipment Rentals	16
		4033	Other Related Rentals	16
		4040	Equipment Repairs	16
		4041	Spa Equipment Repairs	16
		4043	Foodservice Equipment Repairs	16
		4045	Fitness Equipment Repairs	16
		4047	Other Equipment Repairs	16
		4050	Grounds and Landscaping	16
		4060	Heating, Ventilating and Air Conditioning	16
		4061	Electric	16
		4063	Gas	16
		4065	Water	16
		4067	Other HVAC	16
		4070	Locks and Keys	16
		4080	Operating Supplies	16
		4081	Light Bulbs	16
		4083	Small Tools	16
		4085	Equipment Parts	16
		4087	Painting Supplies	16
		4089	Other Operating Supplies	16
		4090	Sauna, Steam and Pool Supplies and Repairs	16
		4091	Repair Materials	16
		4093	Chemicals	16
		4095	Pool Equipment Contracts	16
		4097	Other Sauna, Steam and Pool Repair Costs	16
		4100	Trash Removal	16
		4110	Uniforms	16
		4111	Maintenance Department Employee Uniforms	16
		4113	Uniform Cleaning and Repair	16
		4115	Other Uniform Expenses	16
		4120	Other Repairs and Maintenance	16

Fixed Charges

600	**100**	**1000**	**Fixed Charges**	17
		1100	**Rent**	17
		1110	Land and Building	17
		1120	Other Equipment	17
		1200	**Taxes Other Than Income and Payroll**	17
		1210	Real Estate Taxes	17
		1220	Personal Property Taxes	17
		1230	Business and Occupation Taxes	17
		1240	**Insurance**	17
		1250	Building and Improvements	17
		1260	Liability	17
		1300	**Management Fees**	17
		1400	**Interest Expense**	17
		1410	Mortgages	17
		1420	Notes Payable	17
		1430	Interest on Capital Leases	17
		1440	Other Long-term Debt	17
		1450	Other	17
		1500	**Depreciation and Amortization**	17
		1510	Building and Improvement	17
		1520	Furnishings and Equipment	17
		1530	Leaseholds and Leasehold Improvements	17
		1540	Capital Leases	17
		1550	Other	17
		1600	**Gain (Loss) on Sale of Property**	17

Federal and State Income Taxes

800	**100**	**1000**	**Other Expenses**	18
		1100	**Federal**	18
		1110	Current	18
		1120	Deferred	18
		1200	**State**	18
		1210	Current	18
		1220	Deferred	18

Section 13
Expense Dictionary

This dictionary is designed to help members of the spa industry classify, in accordance with the *Uniform System of Financial Reporting for Spas,* the numerous expense and payroll-related items encountered in their daily work. It will also serve as a ready reference for the spa director, managers, and the persons responsible for purchasing, showing them to which account or expense group the accounting staff will charge each expense item.

It must be noted, however, that not all spa facility expenditures are recorded as expenses. An expenditure made to purchase an item with a useful life of more that one year typically will be capitalized. That is, the amount will be included as an asset on the balance sheet and expensed through depreciation or amortization over the item's useful life. There are some exceptions to this general rule.

The materiality of the expenditure may influence whether the expenditure is capitalized or expensed. Consider, for example, a minor expenditure such as the purchase of an inexpensive treatment room clock for $50. Because this item has a useful life of more than one year, it could be capitalized. However, in this case, the benefit of capitalizing the item may not outweigh the cost of setting up and maintaining the depreciation records. Consequently, the expenditure will likely be expensed. The dollar amount that determines whether expenditures are capitalized or expensed is a matter of judgment. Once the amount is established, it should become part of company or spa policy and be followed consistently.

There are other expenditures that extend the life of an asset or add value to an asset. Generally accepted accounting principles require that these types of expenditures be capitalized and depreciated over the estimated remaining useful life of the asset. The most common example is an expenditure to repair property and equipment. If the repair expenditure only restores the value of the asset to its condition prior to the repair, the expenditure should be expensed. However, if the expenditure extends the life of the asset or increases the value of the asset, the expenditure should be capitalized.

Finally, there are expenditures that are normally expensed, but that, under certain circumstances, are more properly capitalized. Examples include interest costs incurred during the development, construction, or renovation of a property, and the software development costs associated with the purchase of a new computer system. While interest costs and software costs may be expensed in some situations, generally accepted accounting principles prescribe that, when these expenditures are incurred as part of the acquisition of the asset, it is proper to include these expenditures in the total amount that is capitalized. Each spa's controller or accountant should be familiar with the guidelines established by the appropriate accounting principle for the treatment of these or other similar expenditures.

How to Read the Expense Dictionary

GUIDE TO ABBREVIATIONS

Abbreviation	Department/Function/Item
A&G	Administrative and General
Acct. Exp.	Accounting Expense(s)
CGS&L	China, Glassware, Silver, and Linen
Depr. & Amort.	Depreciation and Amortization
Equip. & Supp.	Equipment and Supplies
F&B	Food and Beverages
FM&U	Facility Maintenance and Utilities
HR	Human Resources
HVAC	Heating, Ventilating, and Air Conditioning
IOE	Indirect Operating Expenses
Lease. & Imp.	Leaseholds and Leasehold Improvements
Mktg.	Marketing
OOD	Other Operated Departments
Prof. Prod.	Professional Products and Supplies
PTEB	Payroll Taxes and Employee Benefits
R&M	Repairs and Maintenance
SS&P	Sauna, Steam, and Pool

The Expense Dictionary is divided into two columns. Column I lists expense items alphabetically. Column II identifies the accounts to which the expense items would be charged. Items purchased for direct sale in any department are not included, since their distribution is direct to the cost of goods sold for the department concerned, such as for the food and beverage and retail departments. Column II lists expense accounts in a number of ways. The following is a short explanation of the various forms these listings can take.

If a department, operational function, or cost center is followed by a dash, the entry following the dash is the account charged. For example, the entry **Bathroom Tissue** is **Indirect Operating Expenses—Guest Supplies.** Some expenses are broken down further. The entry for **Depreciation—Building** is **Fixed Charges—Depreciation and Amortization—Building & Improvements.**

If two or three departments or cost centers can charge a particular expense to accounts with the same name, the departments or cost centers are separated by diagonal slashes. For example, the entry for **Hair Bands** is **Hair/Skin Care—Professional Products and Supplies,** as the item is used in both departments. The person coding the invoice for this particular item must determine if the hair bands purchased will be used by the hair department or the skin care department, or whether a portion of the expense should be coded to each account. If more than three departments or cost centers can charge a particular expense to accounts with the same name, the entry will identify the departmental schedule with the generic term **Department.** For example, the entry for **Answering**

Machines is **Department—Telecommunications.** The person coding the invoice for this item must determine to which department the expense pertains.

If the same item is charged by different departments or cost centers to different accounts, departments and accounts are listed consecutively and separated by semicolons. For example, the entry for **Hair Dryers** is **Indirect Operating Expenses—Guest Supplies; Hair—Professional Products and Supplies.** The placement of this expense will depend on whether the hair dryers will be used in the guest grooming areas of the spa or by the hair stylists.

In some instances, an item may apply to more than one account on the same schedule, depending on its use or function. In this case, the department or cost center will be followed by a dash and the relevant accounts separated by a diagonal slash. For example, the entry for **Printed Forms** is **Administrative and General—Operating Supplies/Human Resources.** Printed forms used for human resources purposes go in one account and printed forms for all other purposes go in the other account.

Note: For resort and destination spas, the undistributed operating expense categories of Administrative and General, Marketing, and Facility Maintenance and Utilities do *not* appear on the *spa* section of the overall financial statement, but rather on the corresponding support schedules for the entire property. Thus, when this Expense Dictionary classifies an expense to one of these three undistributed operating expense categories, that expense for resort and destination spas will actually appear on the Summary Statement of Income for the entire property and not on the spa summary page of the statement.

Expense Dictionary

Item	Classification
	A
Accountant's Fees	A&G—Acct. Exp.—Audit & Other External Exp.
Adding Machine Tape	A&G—Operating Supplies
Advertising Agency Fees	Mktg.—Agency Fees
Advertising Direct Mail	Mktg.—Direct Mail
Advertising Directories	Mktg.—Advertising Print
Advertising Outdoor	Mktg.—Other
Advertising Publications	Mktg.—Advertising Print
Advertising Radio and Television	Mktg.—Advertising Broadcast
Agency Fees, Marketing and PR	Mktg.—Agency Fees
Air Conditioning System Repairs	FM&U—HVAC
Airport Transportation for Guests	IOE—Other
Alarm Systems—Fire or Burglar	A&G—Security
Amortization—Mortgage Expense	Fixed Charges—Interest Exp.—Mortgages
Amortization—Leasehold Improvements	Fixed Charges—Depr. & Amort.—Lease. & Imp.
Answering Machines	Department—Telecommunications
Appointment Books	IOE—Operating Supplies

Item	Classification
Aprons	IOE—Guest Supplies; F&B—Uniforms
Armored Car Service	A&G—Contract Services
Aromatherapy Diffusers	IOE—Ambience
Aromatherapy Oils	IOE—Ambience; Massage—Prof. Prod.
ASCAP	Department—Licenses & Fees
Association Dues	Department—Dues & Subscriptions
Attorney's Fees	A&G—Legal & Professional
Audit Fees	A&G—Acct. Exp.—Audit & Other External Exp.
Auto Rental	A&G/Mktg.—Travel
Auto/Truck Repairs	FM&U—Other R&M
Awards—Employee	A&G—HR
Awards—Member	Mktg.—Other
Awnings—Cleaning	FM&U—Contract Services
B	
Background Checks	A&G—HR
Background Music	IOE/Fitness—Ambience
Bad Debts	A&G—Provision for Doubtful Accounts
Bags—Laundry	IOE—Laundry
Bags—Retail	Retail—Gift Wrap & Packaging
Bags—Trash	Department—Operating Supplies
Bank Checks/Charges	A&G—Bank Charges
Barbicide	IOE—Guest Supplies
Barbicide Jars	IOE—Guest Supplies
Bar Utensils	F&B—Utensils
Basket Liners	IOE—Operating Supplies
Bath Mats	IOE/Fitness—Linen
Bath Sheets	IOE—Linen
Bathing Caps	IOE/Fitness—Guest Supplies
Bathroom Tissue	IOE—Guest Supplies
Batteries	IOE/FM&U—Operating Supplies
Beeper/Pager Rental	Department—Telecommunications
Beverage Licenses	F&B—Licenses & Fees
Beverage Stirrers	IOE—Hospitality; F&B—Operating Supplies
Bicycle—Repair	FM&U—Equipment Repair
Billboard Advertising	Mktg.—Other
Billing Statements/Invoices	A&G—Acct. Exp.—Other Acct. Exp.
Binders	A&G—Operating Supplies
Blankets	IOE—Linen
Blankets—Cleaning	IOE—Laundry
Blow Dryers (Hair)	IOE—Guest Supplies: Hair—Prof. Prod.
BMI—Broadcast Music Incorporated	Department—Licenses & Fees
Body Treatment Supplies	Massage—Prof. Prod.
Boiler Inspection	FM&U—HVAC
Boiler Licenses	FM&U—Licenses & Fees
Boiler Repairs	FM&U—HVAC

Item	Classification
Books—Employee Training	Department—Prof. Development
Books—Resource	Department—Dues & Subscriptions
Booth—Trade Show	Mktg.—Trade Shows
Bottle Openers	F&B—Utensils; IOE—Hospitality
Bottled Water	IOE/Fitness—Hospitality
Bowls—Mixing	F&B—Utensils
Bowls—Serving	F&B—CGS&L; IOE—Hospitality
Bowls—Treatment	IOE—Prof. Prod.
Bread and Butter Plates	F&B—CGS&L
Brochures	Mktg.—Collateral Materials
Brushes—Cleaning	IOE—Operating Supplies
Brushes—Hair	IOE—Guest Supplies; Hair—Prof. Prod.
Building and Contents Insurance	Fixed Charges—Insurance Exp.—Building & Improvements
Building Repairs	FM&U—Building
Bulletin Board Supplies	A&G—HR
Burglar Alarm Service	A&G—Security
Business Cards	Department—Operating Supplies
C	
Cable Television Service	Fitness—Ambience
Calculators	Department—Operating Supplies
Calendars	Department—Operating Supplies
Camera and Film—Events	Mktg.—Special Events
Camera Security	A&G—Security
Candles	IOE—Ambience
Caps (Salon)	Hair—Prof. Prod.
Carafes	F&B—CGS&L; IOE—Hospitality
Card Reader Machines	A&G—Acct. Exp.—Other Acct. Exp.
Cardboard Boxes	Retail—Gift Wrap & Packaging
Carpet Repairs	FM&U—Building
Carpet Sweepers	IOE—Operating Supplies
Cartridges—Printer	Department—Operating Supplies
Carts/Trolleys	Department—Operating Supplies
Cash Boxes	A&G—Acct. Exp.—Other Acct. Exp.
Cash Over/Shortage	A&G—Cash Over/Short
Cashier Envelopes	A&G—Acct. Exp.—Other Acct. Exp.
Ceiling Repair	FM&U—Building
Cellular Phone Charges	Department—Telecommunications
Chamber of Commerce Dues	A&G—Dues & Subscriptions
Charge Vouchers	A&G—Other Accounting Expense
Checks/Checking Supplies	A&G—Acct. Exp.—Other Acct. Exp.
Chemicals—Cleaning	IOE—Operating Supplies
Chemicals—Laundry	Department—Laundry
Chemicals—Pool	FM&U—SS&P Supp. & Rep.
China	F&B—CGS&L; IOE—Hospitality
Christmas Gifts—Employee	Department—PTEB
Christmas Gifts—Others	A&G/Mktg.—Other

Item	Classification
Christmas Trees and Decorations	IOE—Ambience
Civic and Community Activities	Mktg.—Special Events
Cleaning—Contract	Department—Contract Services
Cleaning Supplies	Department—Operating Supplies
Cleansing Pads	Skin Care—Prof. Prod. & Supp
Clipboards	IOE—Operating Supplies
Clips (Hair)	Hair—Prof. Prod. & Supp
Clock (Treatment Room)	IOE—Operating Supplies
Coat Hangers	IOE—Guest Supplies
Coffee—Hospitality	IOE—Hospitality
Coffee Pots	F&B—Operating Supplies; IOE—Hospitality
Coffee—Supplies	F&B—Operating Supplies; IOE—Hospitality
Coin Handling Supplies	A&G—Acct. Exp.—Other Acct. Exp.
Collection Fees	A&G—Credit & Collection
Combs	IOE—Guest Supplies; Hair—Prof. Prod.
Comedone Extractor	Skin Care—Prof. Prod.
Commissions—Travel Agent	Mktg.—Other
Compact Discs	IOE/Fitness—Ambience
Complimentary Beverages	IOE/Fitness—Hospitality
Complimentary Food	IOE—Hospitality
Computers	A&G—Information Systems
Computer—Capital Lease	Fixed Charges—Interest Exp.—Interest on Capital Leases
Computer—Operating Lease	IOE/Fitness/Retail—Equip. Rental; A&G—Information Systems
Computer Printer Paper	Department—Operating Supplies
Computer—Repair	FM&U—Equipment Repair
Computer Tech Support	A&G—Information Systems
Computer Software	A&G—Information Systems
Conditioner—Amenity	IOE/Fitness—Guest Supplies
Conditioner—Professional	Hair—Prof. Prod.
Consultant Fees, Professional	A&G—Legal & Professional
Contact Lens Solution	IOE—Guest Supplies
Contract Cleaning	Department—Contract Services
Contract Entertainment	IOE/Fitness—Ambience
Contract Exterminating	FM&U—Contract Services
Contributions	A&G—Donations
Copier Paper	A&G—Operating Supplies
Copier Rental	Fixed Charges—Interest Exp.—Interest on Capital Leases
Copier Toner	A&G—Operating Supplies
Copying Service	A&G—Other; Mktg.—Direct Mail
Copyright and Trademark Licenses	A&G—Licenses & Fees
Corkscrews	F&B—Utensils
Cosmetic Supplies	Hair/OOD (Make-Up)—Prof. Prod.

Item	Classification
Cotton Balls/Pads	Skin Care/Nail—Prof. Prod.; IOE—Guest Supplies
Cotton Swabs	Skin Care/Nail—Prof. Prod.; IOE—Guest Supplies
Credit Card Discount Fees	A&G—Credit Card Commissions
Credit and Collection Expense	A&G—Credit & Collection
Credit Reports	A&G—Acct. Exp.—Other Acct. Exp.
Cups—China	F&B—CGS&L; IOE—Hospitality
Cups—Paper	F&B—Operating Supplies; IOE—Hospitality
Curling Irons	Hair—Prof. Prod.; IOE—Guest Supplies
Curtains—Cleaning	Department—Contract Services
Curtains—Shower/Dressing Rooms	IOE/Fitness—Operating Supplies
D	
Damaged Articles	A&G—Loss & Damage
Decorating and Painting	FM&U—Other
Decorations	IOE—Ambience
Deodorants—Amenity	IOE/Fitness—Guest Supplies
Deodorizers	IOE/Fitness—Ambience
Depreciation—Building	Fixed Charges—Depr. & Amort.—Building & Improvements
Depreciation—Equipment	Fixed Charges—Depr. & Amort.—Furnishings & Equipment
Desk Accessories	Department—Operating Supplies
Detail Tape	A&G—Acct. Exp.—Other Acct. Exp.
Detective Services—Consultative	A&G—Security
Detergents—Laundry	Department—Laundry
Direct Mail Expenses—Outside Services	Mktg.—Direct Mail
Directional Signs	FM&U—Building
Directories—Reference	Department—Dues & Subscriptions
Directory Advertising	Mktg.—Advertising Print
Dishes—China	F&B—CGS&L; IOE—Hospitality
Dishes—Paper	F&B—Operating Supplies; IOE—Hospitality
Dishwasher Repairs	FM&U—Equipment Repair
Dishwashing—Chemicals	F&B/IOE—Operating Supplies
Disinfectants	Department—Operating Supplies
Dispensers, Shower	IOE/Fitness—Guest Supplies
Display—Fixtures, Retail	Retail—Merchandise Displays & Accessories
Display Rack—Magazine	IOE/Fitness—Guest Supplies
Disposable Apparel	IOE—Guest Supplies
Donations	A&G—Donations
Doubtful Accounts	A&G—Provision for Doubtful Accounts
Drapery Cleaning	Department—Contract Services
Drinking Glasses	F&B—CGS&L; IOE—Hospitality
Drugs and Medical Supplies—Employee	A&G—HR

Item	Classification
Drugs and Medical Supplies—Guest	Department—Guest Supplies
Drug Testing Service	A&G—HR
Dryers—Hair	Hair—Prof Prod.; IOE—Guest Supplies
Dryers—Nail	Nail—Prof. Prod.
Dues—Association	Department—Dues & Subscriptions
Dust Cloths	IOE—Operating Supplies
DVDs and Players	Fitness—Ambience
E	
Educational Books—Employees	Department—Prof. Development
Educational Programs—Employee	Department—Prof. Development
Educational Programs—Guest	Health & Wellness—Prof. Prod.
Electric Blankets and Pads	IOE—Linen
Electric Bulbs	FM&U—Operating Supplies
Electric—Utilities	FM&U—Utility Exp.—Electric
Elevator Maintenance Contract	FM&U—Contract Services
Employee Background Checks	A&G—HR
Employee Housing	A&G—HR
Employee Meals	Department—PTEB
Employee Records—Supplies	A&G—HR
Employee Relations Expenses	Department—PTEB
Employment Agency Fees	A&G—HR
Engineering Supplies	FM&U—Operating Supplies
Entertainment and Music	IOE/Fitness—Ambience
Envelopes	Department—Operating Supplies
Epilating Strips	Skin Care—Prof. Prod.
Essential Oils	Massage—Prof Prod.; IOE—Ambience
Exchange on Bank Checks and Currency	Rentals & Other Income—Foreign Currency Transactions
Executive Office Expense	A&G—Corporate Office Charges
Exercise Accessories	Fitness—Athletic Equipment & Supplies
Express Delivery Charges	A&G—Postage; Retail—Packaging & Freight
Extension Cords	FM&U—Operating Supplies
Extraction Utensils	Skin Care—Prof. Prod.
Eye Pillow	Massage/Skin Care—Prof. Prod.
F	
Face Cloths	IOE—Linen
Face Cradle Covers	Massage—Prof. Prod.
Facial Brushes	Skin Care—Prof Prod.
Facial Headwear	Skin Care—Prof. Prod.
Facial Mirror	Skin Care—Prof. Prod.
Facial Tissue	IOE—Guest Supplies, Skin Care—Prof. Prod.
Facial Treatment Professional Products	Skin Care—Prof. Prod.
Facial Treatment Supplies	Skin Care—Prof. Prod.
Fax Machine Supplies and Accessories	A&G—Operating Supplies

Item	Classification
Federal Income Taxes	Federal & State Income Taxes—Federal
Fees, Attorneys for Collection	A&G—Credit & Collection
Fees, Attorneys for Other than Collection	A&G—Legal & Professional
Fees, Audit	A&G—Acct. Exp.—Audit & Other External Exp.
Fees, Franchise	Mktg—Other
Fees, Legal	A&G—Legal & Professional
Fees, Management	Fixed Charges—Management Fees
Fees Notary	A&G—Legal & Professional
Fees, Stock Transfer Agents	A&G—Legal & Professional
Fees, Trustees	A&G—Legal & Professional
FICA	Department—PTEB
File Boxes	A&G—Acct. Exp.—Other Acct. Exp.
File Cabinets	A&G—Operating Supplies
Film Purchase and Development	Mktg.—Special Events
Films—Entertainment	IOE/Fitness—Ambience
Fire Alarm System Maintenance	FM&U—Contract Services
First Aid Supplies	A&G—HR; Department—Guest Supplies
Fitness Equipment Accessories	Fitness—Athletic Equip. & Supplies
Flatware—Metal	F&B—CGS&L; IOE—Hospitality
Flatware—Plastic	F&B—Operating Supplies; IOE—Hospitality
Fleece Table Pads	IOE—Guest Supplies
Floor Finish	IOE—Operating Supplies
Floor Mats, Relief	IOE—Operating Supplies
Floor Mats, Walk Off	FM&U—Operating Supplies
Floor Mats, Wet Rooms	IOE—Operating Supplies
Floor Plans	FM&U—Building
Flowers	IOE—Ambience
Flyers	Mktg.—In-House Promotions
Foam Applicators	Skin Care—Prof. Prod.
Foil Wrapping	F&B—Operating Supplies; Hair—Prof. Prod.
Food—Hospitality	IOE—Hospitality
Food Licenses	F&B—Licenses and Fees
Forks—Metal	F&B—CGS&S; IOE—Hospitality
Forks—Plastic	F&B—Operating Supplies; IOE—Hospitality
Forms Printed or General	A&G—Operating Supplies
Fountains, Water Feature	IOE—Ambience
Franchise Fees	Mktg.—Other
Free Weights	Fitness—Athletic Equip. & Supplies
Freight Charges—Outbound	Retail—Packaging & Freight
Fruit—Hospitality	IOE—Hospitality
Fuel—Gas	FM&U—Utility Exp.—Gas
Fuel—Kitchen	F&B—Operating Supplies
Fuel—Oil Heating	FM&U—Utility Exp.—Other
Furniture Polish	IOE—Operating Supplies

Item	Classification
Furniture Rental	Fixed Charges—Interest Exp.—Interest on Capital Leases
Furniture Repairs	FM&U—Other R&M
FUTA	Department—PTEB
G	
Garbage Removal	FM&U—Trash Removal
Garment Checks, Printed	IOE—Operating Supplies
Gas Cooking—Propane	F&B—Operating Supplies
Gas—Heating	FM&U—Utility Exp.—Gas
Gasoline	A&G/Mktg.—Travel; FM&U—Other
Gauze, First Aid	A&G—HR; Department—Guest Supplies
Gauze, Treatment	Skin Care—Prof. Prod.
Gift Boxes	Retail—Gift Wrap & Packaging
Gift Cards	Mktg.—Collateral Material
Gift Certificates	Mktg.—Collateral Material
Glass Amenity Containers	IOE—Guest Supplies
Glass Bowls	F&B—CGS&L; IOE—Hospitality
Glass Dishes	F&B—CGS&L; IOE—Hospitality
Glass Serviceware	F&B—CGS&L; IOE—Hospitality
Glasses, Drinking	F&B—CGS&L; IOE—Hospitality
Glassware, Treatment	Department—Prof. Prod.
Gloves, Treatment	Department—Prof. Prod.
Grooming Area Product Displays	IOE—Guest Supplies
Grounds Expense	FM&U—Grounds & Landscaping
H	
Hair Bands	Hair/Skin Care—Prof. Prod.
Hair Clips	Hair—Prof. Prod.
Hair Dryers	IOE—Guest Supplies; Hair—Prof. Prod.
Hair Grooming Supplies	Hair—Prof Prod.; IOE—Guest Supplies
Hair Nets	Department—Uniforms
Hair—Professional Products	Hair—Prof. Prod.
Hair Removal Supplies	Skin Care—Prof. Prod.
Hair Ties	Hair—Prof. Prod.
Hairspray—Amenity	Department—Guest Supplies
Hairspray—Salon	Hair—Prof. Prod.
Hand and Foot Treatment Supplies	Nail—Prof. Prod.
Hand Mits	Massage/Skin Care—Prof. Prod.
Hand Soap, Employee	Department—Operating Supplies
Hand Soap, Guest	Department—Guest Supplies
Hand Towels	Department—Linen
Hand Weights	Fitness—Athletic Equip. & Supplies
Hangers	Department—Guest Supplies
Heat Lamps	Department—Prof. Prod.
Heat Packs, Treatment	Massage—Prof. Prod.
Heating Booties/Mitts	Skin Care/Nail—Prof. Prod.

Item	Classification
Help Wanted Ads	A&G—HR
Herbal Wrap Sheets	Massage—Prof. Prod.
Hoses, Garden	FM&U—Grounds & Landscaping
Hoses, Utility	FM&U—Operating Supplies
Hotel Association Dues	A&G—Dues & Subscriptions
Hotel Sales and Marketing Association Dues	Mktg.—Dues & Subscriptions
Hot Rollers	Hair—Prof. Prod.; IOE—Guest Supplies
Hot Towel Cabinet	Department—Prof. Prod.
House Publications—Employee	A&G—HR
Housing—Employee	A&G—HR
Hydrotherapy Supplies	Massage—Prof. Prod.
I	
Ice/Ice Buckets	F&B—Operating Supplies; IOE—Hospitality
Income Taxes	Federal & State Income Taxes—Federal/State
Independent Research Firm Fees	A&G/Mktg.—Legal & Professional
Infrared Lamps	Hair—Prof. Prod.
Ink Pads	IOE—Operating Supplies; A&G—Acct. Exp.—Other Acct. Exp.
Insecticides	FM&U—Other R&M
Inside Signage	Mktg.—In-House Promotions; FM&U—Building
Instrument Disinfectant	Department—Prof. Prod.
Insurance—Building and Contents	Fixed Charges—Insurance—Building & Improvements
Insurance—Dental	Department—PTEB
Insurance—Fire	Fixed Charges—Insurance—Building & Improvements
Insurance—General	Fixed Charges—Insurance—Building & Improvements
Insurance—Liability	Fixed Charges—Insurance—Liability
Insurance—Life	Department—PTEB
Insurance—Medical	Department—PTEB
Insurance—Workman's Compensation	Department—PTEB
Interest—Mortgages	Fixed Charges—Interest Exp.—Mortgages
Interest—Notes	Fixed Charges—Interest Exp.—Notes Payable
Internet Telephone Charge	Department—Telecommunications
Internet Web Site	Mktg.—Advertising Broadcast
Interview Expense	A&G—HR
J	
Janitorial Cleaning Service	Department—Contract Services
Jewelry Cleaner	IOE—Guest Supplies
Juices—Hospitality	IOE—Hospitality

Item	Classification
K	
Knives—Dining	F&B—CGS&L; IOE—Hospitality
Knives—Kitchen	F&B—Utensils
Knives—Plastic	F&B—Operating Supplies; IOE—Hospitality
L	
Lab Coats	Department—Uniforms
Labels	A&G—Operating Supplies
Ladles	F&B—Utensils
Lancets	Skin Care—Prof. Prod.
Landscaping	FM&U—Grounds & Landscaping
Lash, Perms and Tints Supplies	Hair—Prof. Prod.
Laundry—In-House, Chemicals	Department—Laundry
Laundry—In-House, Supplies	Department—Laundry
Laundry—Outside Service	Department—Laundry
Leasehold Improvements Amortization	Fixed Charges—Depr. & Amort.—Lease. & Imp.
Legal Expense and Fees	A&G—Legal & Professional
Licenses, Beverage	F&B/IOE—Licenses & Fees
Licenses, Boiler	FM&U—Licenses & Fees
Licenses, Elevator	FM&U—Licenses & Fees
Licenses, Engineering	FM&U—Licenses & Fees
Licenses, General	A&G—Licenses & Fees
Licenses, Gift Shop	Retail—Licenses & Fees
Licenses, Trademark and Copyright	A&G—Licenses & Fees
Life Jackets	Fitness—Athletic Equip. & Supplies
Light Bulbs	FM&U—Operating Supplies
Linen	IOE—Linen
Linen Carts	IOE—Laundry
Linen Napkins	F&B—CGS&L; IOE—Hospitality
Linen Rental	F&B—CGS&L; IOE—Linen
Linen Terry Cloth	IOE—Linen
Liners	IOE—Operating Supplies
Lobby Cleaning Contract	IOE—Contract Services
Lock Box Services	A&G—Bank Charges
Locker Repairs	FM&U—Equipment Repair
Locker Room Amenities	Fitness/IOE—Guest Supplies
Locker Room Supplies	Fitness/IOE—Guest Supplies
Locks and Keys	FM&U—Locks & Keys
Log Books	Fitness/IOE—Operating Supplies
Long Distance Telephone Charges	Department—Telecommunications
Loofah	Massage—Prof. Prod.
Lost and Damaged Articles	A&G—Loss & Damage

Item	Classification
M	
Magazine Advertising	Mktg.—Advertising Print
Magnifying Lamps	Skin Care/Nail—Prof. Prod.; IOE—Guest Supplies
Mailing Lists	Mktg.—Direct Mail
Maintenance Contracts—Computers	A&G—Information Systems
Maintenance Contracts—Electric Signs	FM&U—Contract Services
Maintenance Contracts—Fitness Equipment	Fitness—Contract Services
Maintenance Contracts—Office Equipment	FM&U—Contract Services
Maintenance Contracts—Telephone Equipment	FM&U—Contract Services
Make-up Supplies	Hair/Other (Make-up)—Prof. Prod.
Management Fees	Fixed Charges—Management Fees
Manicure Supplies	Nail—Prof. Prod.
Mannequins	Retail—Merchandise Displays & Accessories
Manuals—Service	FM&U—Other R&M
Marketing Fees	Mktg.—Agency Fees
Masque Brush	Skin Care—Prof. Prod.
Massage, Bolsters	Massage—Prof. Prod
Massage, Bottles	Massage—Prof. Prod.
Massage, Oils	Massage—Prof. Prod.
Massage, Treatment Supplies	Massage—Prof. Prod.
Matches	IOE—Guest Supplies
Mats, Anti-Fatigue	IOE—Operating Supplies
Mats, Bath	IOE/Fitness—Linen
Mats, Fitness	Fitness—Operating Supplies
Mats, Floor	FM&U—Operating Supplies
Mats, Locker Room	FM&U—Operating Supplies
Meals—Employee	Department—PTEB
Meals and Entertainment	A&G/Mktg.—Meals & Entertainment
Measuring Beakers/Cups	Massage/Hair—Prof. Prod.
Medical Supplies	IOE—Guest Supplies; A&G—HR
Medicine Balls	Fitness—Athletic Equip. & Supplies
Member Publications	Mktg.—Other
Membership Applications	Mktg.—Collateral Materials
Membership Camera and Film	Mktg.—Special Events
Membership Dues—Association	Department—Dues & Subscriptions
Menus	F&B—Other; Mktg.—Collateral Materials
Merchandise Bags	Retail—Gift Wrap & Packaging
Metal Polish	Department—Operating Supplies
Microdermabrasion Supplies	Skin Care—Prof. Prod.
Mirrors, Hand	Hair/Skin Care—Prof. Prod.
Mirrors, Make-up	IOE—Guest Supplies
Mitts and Liners	Skin Care/Nail—Prof. Prod.

Item	Classification
Mixing Bowls	F&B—Utensils; IOE—Operating Supplies
Mixing Spoons	F&B—Utensils; IOE—Operating Supplies
Moisturizer/Body Lotion—Amenity	IOE—Guest Supplies
Mops, Handles and Wringers	Department—Operating Supplies
Mortgage—Interest	Fixed Charges—Interest Exp.—Mortgages
Motor Repair	FM&U—Equipment Repair
Mouthwash—Amenity	Department—Guest Supplies
Mouthwash Cups	Department—Guest Supplies
Mud Products	Massage—Prof. Prod.
Municipal Licenses	A&G—Licenses & Fees
Music Licenses	Department—Licenses & Fees
Music Tapes/CDs	IOE/Fitness—Ambience
Musicians	IOE—Ambience
N	
Nail Supplies	Nail—Prof. Prod.
Name Badges	Department—Operating Supplies
Napkins—Linen	F&B—CGS&L; IOE—Hospitality
Napkins—Paper	F&B—Operating Supplies; IOE—Hospitality
Newsletters	Mktg.—Other
Newspapers	IOE—Guest Supplies
Notary Fees	A&G—Legal & Professional
O	
Office Supplies and Accessories	Department—Operating Supplies
Oil/Lotion Warmers	Massage—Prof. Prod.
Outdoor Advertising	Mktg.—Other
Overages and Shortages in Cash	A&G—Cash Over/Short
P	
Packaging/Private Label Development	Retail—Gift Wrap & Packaging
Packing Supplies	Retail—Packaging & Freight
Pager Rentals	Department—Telecommunications
Paint	FM&U—Operating Supplies
Paint Solvents	FM&U—Operating Supplies
Pamphlets	Mktg.—Collateral Materials
Paper Bags	Retail—Gift Wrap & Packaging
Paper Clips	A&G—Operating Supplies
Paper for Copiers	A&G—Operating Supplies
Paper Liners	IOE—Operating Supplies
Paper Napkins	F&B—Operating Supplies; IOE—Hospitality
Paper for Printers	Department—Operating Supplies
Paper Slippers	Nail—Prof. Prod.
Paper Towels	IOE—Guest Supplies
Paraffin	Skin Care/Nail—Prof. Prod.
Paraffin Baths	Nail—Prof. Prod.

Item	Classification
Party Favors	F&B—Banquet & Party Costs; Mktg.—Special Events
Party Supplies	F&B—Banquet & Party Costs; Mktg.—Special Events
Pastry Bags	F&B—Operating Supplies
Payroll Processing Service	A&G—Acct. Exp.—Payroll Processing Exp.
Pedicure Supplies	Nail—Prof. Prod.
Pencil Sharpeners	A&G—Operating Supplies
Pencils	A&G—Operating Supplies
Pens	A&G—Operating Supplies
Pensions	Department—PTEB
Perm Rods	Hair—Prof. Prod.
Personal Property Taxes	Fixed Charges—Taxes—Personal Property Taxes
Personnel Forms	A&G—HR
Pest Control	FM&U—Contract Services
Photography	Mktg.—Other
Plastic Bottles	Department—Prof. Prod.
Plastic Liners (Heat, Mitts)	Nail/Skin Care—Prof. Prod.
Plastic Wrap, Body Treatment	Massage—Prof. Prod.
Plates	F&B—CGS&L; IOE—Hospitality
Platters	F&B—CGS&L; IOE—Hospitality
Plumbing Repairs	FM&U—Other R&M
Point-of-Sale Repair	FM&U—Equipment Repair
Polishes (Furniture)	IOE—Operating Supplies
Polishes (Nail)	Nail—Prof. Prod.
Pool Accessories	FM&U—SS&P Supplies & Repairs
Pool Chemicals	FM&U—SS&P Supplies & Repairs
Pool Repair and Maintenance	FM&U—SS&P Supplies & Repairs
Pool Towels	IOE/Fitness—Linen
Post Office Box Rental	A&G—Postage
Postage	A&G—Postage
Postage Machine Rental	A&G—Postage
Postage for Promotional Mailings	Mktg.—Direct Mail
Postcards	Mktg.—Collateral Materials
Posters—Safety	A&G—HR
Potpourri	IOE—Ambience
Printed Forms	A&G—Operating Supplies/HR
Printer Supplies and Accessories	Department—Operating Supplies
Printing and Stationery	A&G—Operating Supplies
Prizes—Employee	A&G—HR
Prizes—Member	Mktg.—Special Events
Professional Body Care Products	Massage—Prof. Prod.
Professional Hair Products	Hair—Prof. Prod.
Professional Make-up	Hair/OOD (Make-up)—Prof. Prod.
Professional Massage Products	Massage—Prof. Prod.
Professional Nail Products	Nail—Prof. Prod.
Professional Skin Care Products	Skin Care—Prof. Prod.

Item	Classification
Protective Services (Security)	A&G—Security
Provision for Doubtful Accounts	A&G—Provision for Doubtful Accounts
Public Area Cleaning Service	IOE—Contract Services
Public Liability Insurance	Fixed Charges—Insurance—Liability
Public Relations Agency	Mktg.—Agency Fees
Publications—Employee	A&G—HR
Publications—Member	Mktg.—Other
Pump Repairs	FM&U—Equipment Repair
Q	
Q-Tips	IOE—Guest Supplies
R	
Razors	IOE—Guest Supplies; Hair—Prof. Prod.
Reading Racks	IOE—Guest Supplies
Real Estate Rent (Land and Buildings)	Fixed Charges—Rent—Land & Buildings
Real Estate Taxes	Fixed Charges—Taxes—Real Estate Taxes
Record Books	A&G—Operating Supplies
Recruitment—Employee	A&G—HR
Recycle Bins	IOE—Operating Supplies
Refrigeration Maintenance and Supplies	FM&U—Other R&M
Refuse Removal	FM&U—Trash Removal
Registration Cards	IOE—Operating Supplies
Registration—Internet Address	A&G—Legal & Professional
Rent—Building and Land	Fixed Charges—Rent—Land & Buildings
Rent Computer Equipment	A&G—Information Systems
Rent—Fitness Equipment	Fitness—Equipment Rental
Rent—Furniture	Fixed Charges—Interest Exp.—Interest on Capital Leases
Rent—Office Equipment	A&G—Other
Rental Banquet Tables and Chairs	F&B—Banquet & Party Costs; Mktg.—Special Events
Restaurant Checks	F&B—Operating Supplies
Restaurant Signs	Mktg.—In-House Promotions
Retail Bags	Retail—Gift Wrap & Packaging
Retail Displays and Fixtures	Retail—Merchandise Displays & Accessories
Ring Binders	A&G—Operating Supplies
Robes	IOE—Guest Clothing
Royalties, BMI/ASCAP	Department—Licenses & Fees
Rubber Bands	A&G—Operating Supplies
Rubber Gloves	Department—Prof. Prod.
Rubber Stamps	Department—Operating Supplies
Rubbing Alcohol	Nail—Prof. Prod.
S	
Safe Deposit Box Keys	FM&U—Locks & Keys
Safe Deposit Box Offsite Rental	A&G—Security

Item	Classification
Safety Pins	IOE—Operating Supplies
Sales Checks	IOE/Retail—Operating Supplies
Salon Towels	IOE—Linen
Salts	Massage—Prof. Prod.
Sandals	IOE—Guest Clothing
Sanitation Supplies	Department—Operating Supplies
Saucers	F&B—CGS&L; IOE—Hospitality
Sauna Repairs	FM&U—SS&P Supplies & Repairs
Sauna Supplies	FM&U—SS&P Supplies & Repairs
Scissors	Hair—Prof. Prod.; A&G—Operating Supplies
Scotch Tape	A&G—Operating Supplies
Security Camera	A&G—Security
Security Contracts	A&G—Security
Service Manuals	FM&U—Other R&M
Serving Dishes	F&B—CGS&L; IOE—Hospitality
Sewer	FM&U—Utility Exp.—Water
Shampoo, Amenity	IOE—Guest Supplies
Shampoo, Locker Room	IOE—Guest Supplies
Shampoo, Professional	Hair—Prof. Prod.
Shaving Cream, Amenity	Department—Guest Supplies
Sheets	IOE—Linen
Shipping Fees	Retail—Packaging & Freight
Shoe Cloths	IOE—Guest Supplies
Shortages and Overages of Cash	A&G—Cash Over/Short
Shower Dispensers	IOE—Guest Supplies
Shower Gels—Amenity	Department—Guest Supplies
Sidewalk Repairs and Maintenance	FM&U—Building
Signage	FM&U—Building
Silver Polish	F&B/IOE—Operating Supplies
Smocks (Guest)	IOE—Guest Clothing
Soap, Laundry	Department—Laundry
Soaps, Amenity	Department—Guest Supplies
Social Activities—Employee	A&G—HR
Software Application Upgrades	A&G—Information Systems
Software Leases	A&G—Information Systems
Software Licenses	A&G—Information Systems
Solo Plastic Cups, Pre-measuring	IOE—Operating Supplies
Sound Equipment Repairs	FM&U—Equipment Repair
Spatulas, Treatment	IOE—Operating Supplies
Sponges, Treatment	Skin Care—Prof. Prod.
Spoons, Dining	F&B—CGS&L; IOE—Hospitality
Spoons, Kitchen	F&B—Utensils
Spoons, Plastic	F&B—Operating Supplies; IOE—Hospitality
Sports Equipment and Balls	Fitness—Athletic Equip. & Supplies
Spray Bottles	Department—Prof. Prod.; IOE—Operating Supplies

Item	Classification
Squeegees	IOE—Operating Supplies
Stainless Steel Bowls	Massage/Skin Care—Prof. Prod.
Stairway Repairs	FM&U—Building
Stamps, General	A&G—Operating Supplies
Stamps, Postage	A&G—Postage
Staplers/Staples	A&G—Operating Supplies
State Income Taxes	Federal & State Income Taxes—State
State Unemployment Taxes	Department—PTEB
Stationery	A&G—Operating Supplies
Steam Room Repairs	FM&U—SS&P Supplies & Repairs
Steam Room Supplies	FM&U—SS&P Supplies & Repairs
Steel Wool	F&B/IOE—Operating Supplies
Steps Fitness	Fitness—Athletic Equip. & Supplies
Stereo Equipment	IOE/Fitness—Ambience
Sterilizers	Department—Prof. Prod.
Sterilizing Containers	IOE—Operating Supplies
Stirrers	F&B—Operating Supplies; IOE—Hospitality
Stock Pots	F&B—Utensils
Stock Transfer Agents—Fees	A&G—Legal & Professional
Stones, Hot	Massage/Skin Care/Nail—Prof. Prod.
Storage of Equipment/Records Off Site	A&G—Other
Storage Files	A&G—Acct. Exp.—Other Acct. Exp.
Strainers	F&B—Utensils
Straws	F&B—Operating Supplies; IOE—Hospitality
Subscriptions for Guests	IOE—Guest Supplies
Subscriptions, Professional	Department—Dues & Subscriptions
Sun Tanning Supplies and Accessories	IOE—Other
Surge Protector	FM&U—Other R&M
Surgical Gloves	Department—Prof. Prod.
Swimming Pool Repairs	FM&U—SS&P Supplies & Repair
Swimming Suit Bags	IOE/Fitness—Guest Supplies
Swiss Balls	Fitness—Athletic Equip. & Supplies

T

Item	Classification
Table Cloths	F&B—CGS&L
Table Covers (Massage)	IOE—Linen
Table Pads	IOE—Linen
Table Tents	Mktg.—In-House Promotions
Tape, Masking	FM&U—Operating Supplies
Tape, Packing	Retail—Packaging & Freight
Tapes, Cassette and VHS	IOE/Fitness—Ambience
Teapots	F&B—CGS&L; IOE—Hospitality
Technical Books	Department—Prof. Development
Telephone Accessories	Department—Telecommunications
Telephone, Cellular	Department—Telecommunications
Telephone Charges	Department—Telecommunications

Item	Classification
Telephone Directory Advertising	Mktg.—Advertising Print
Telephone Equipment Changes	Department—Telecommunications
Telephone Equipment Rentals	Fixed Charges—Interest Exp.—Interest on Capital Leases
Telephone Line Usage—Computers	Department—Telecommunications
Televisions	Fitness/IOE—Operating Supplies
Timers	IOE—Operating Supplies
Toilet Paper for Guests	IOE—Guest Supplies
Toilet Repair	FM&U—Other R&M
Toner	Department—Operating Supplies
Tour Agency Commissions	Mktg.—Other
Towels	Fitness/IOE—Linen
Trade Magazines and Publications	Department—Dues & Subscriptions
Trade Show Display	Mktg.—Trade Shows
Trademarks	A&G—Licenses & Fees
Training—Employee	Department—Prof. Development
Transfer Fees	A&G—Bank Charges
Trash Removal	FM&U—Trash Removal
Travel Agency Commissions	Mktg.—Other
Travel Expense	A&G/Mktg.—Travel; Retail—Buying Trips
Trays, F&B	F&B—Operating Supplies
Trays, Grooming	IOE—Guest Supplies
Trays, Treatment	IOE—Operating Supplies
Treadmill Accessories	Fitness—Athletic Equip. & Supplies
Trolleys/Carts	Department—Operating Supplies
Turbans	Hair/Skin Care—Prof. Prod.
Tweezers	Skin Care/Hair/Nail—Prof. Prod.
U	
Uncollectible Accounts	A&G—Provision for Doubtful Accounts
Uniforms	Department—Uniforms
Uniform Cleaning	Department—Uniforms
Union (Trade, Insurance & Pension Fund Employer's Contribution)	Department—PTEB
Utensils, Kitchen	F&B—Utensils
V	
Vacuum Cleaner Accessories	FM&U—Equipment Repair
Vacuum Cleaners	IOE—Operating Supplies
Valet Parking Tickets	IOE—Operating Supplies
VCRs	IOE/Health & Wellness/Fitness—Operating Supplies
Video Equipment	Department—Operating Supplies
Vinyl Gloves	IOE—Operating Supplies
Volleyballs and Nets	Fitness—Athletic Equip. & Supplies
Vouchers	A&G—Operating Supplies

Item	Classification
W	
Walk Off Mats	FM&U—Operating Supplies
Want Ads	A&G—HR
Waste Removal	FM&U—Trash Removal
Wastebaskets and Liners	Department—Operating Supplies
Water, Bottled	IOE/Fitness—Hospitality
Water, Distilled	IOE—Operating Supplies
Water and Sewer	FM&U—Utility Exp.—Water
Wax Paper	F&B—Operating Supplies
Waxing Supplies	Skin Care—Prof. Prod.
Weight Hand Grips	Fitness—Athletic Equip. & Supplies
Whirlpool Repairs and Maintenance	FM&U—SS&P Supplies & Repairs
Window Coverings, Cleaning	Department—Contract Services
Window Shades, Screen Awning Repairs	FM&U—Other
Workers' Compensation Insurance	Department—PTEB
Wrapping Paper	Retail—Gift Wrap & Packaging
Wraps, Facial	Skin Care—Prof. Prod.
Wraps, Plastic	Massage—Prof. Prod.
Wringers and Mop Handles	Department—Operating Supplies
Y	
Yoga Mats and Supplies	Fitness—Athletic Equip. & Supplies

Section 14
Sample Income Statement and Supporting Schedules

SUMMARY STATEMENT OF INCOME

	Net Revenues	Cost of Sales	Payroll and Related Expenses	Other Expenses	Income (Loss)
Spa Departments					
Massage	$ 1,446,000	$	$ 829,000	$ 45,000	$ 572,000
Skin Care	523,000		299,500	41,000	182,500
Nail	199,800		108,400	6,600	84,800
Hair	206,000		115,400	10,500	80,100
Total Spa Contributions	2,374,800		1,352,300	103,100	919,400
Indirect Expenses					
Indirect Support Labor			255,200		255,200
Indirect Operating Expenses				190,000	190,000
Total Indirect Expenses			255,200	190,000	445,200
Spa After Indirect Expenses	2,374,800		1,607,500	293,100	474,200
Memberships	174,000				174,000
Other Operated Departments					
Fitness	198,800		200,900	22,900	(25,000)
Food and Beverage	99,000	32,100	44,800	18,000	4,100
Retail	515,600	268,000	108,600	22,700	116,300
Rentals and Other Income	58,500				58,500
Total Operated Departmental Contributions	871,900	300,100	354,300	63,600	153,900
Income Before Undistributed Expenses	3,420,700	300,100	1,961,800	356,700	802,100
Undistributed Operating Expenses					
Administrative and General			101,300	65,300	166,600
Marketing			34,200	64,900	99,100
Facilities Maintenance and Utilities			0	128,000	128,000
Total Undistributed Operating Expenses			135,500	258,200	393,700
Income Before Fixed Charges	$ 3,420,700	$ 300,100	$ 2,097,300	$ 614,900	$ 408,400
Fixed Charges					89,000
Income Before Depreciation, Amortization, Interest and Income Taxes					319,400
Depreciation and Amortization					80,000
Interest Expense					30,000
Gain or Loss on Disposal of Property					(50,000)
Income Before Income Taxes					259,400
Income Taxes					75,000
Net Income					$ 184,400

Massage

	Current Period
REVENUE	
Massage	
Relaxation and Therapeutic	$ 855,000
Specialty	285,000
Total Massage	1,140,000
Body Treatments	
Hydrotherapy	10,000
Wraps and Scrubs	80,000
Specialty Body Treatments	45,000
Total Body Treatments	135,000
Other	
Breakage	5,000
Service Charges	170,000
Other Revenue	10,000
Total Other	185,000
TOTAL REVENUE	1,460,000
ALLOWANCES	14,000
NET REVENUE	1,446,000
DIRECT EXPENSES	
Payroll and Related Expenses	
Salaries and Wages	90,000
Commissions	412,000
Contract	38,000
Distributed Service Charges	140,000
Payroll Taxes and Employee Benefits	149,000
Total Payroll and Related Expenses	829,000
Other—Professional Products and Supplies	45,000
TOTAL DIRECT EXPENSES	874,000
DEPARTMENTAL CONTRIBUTION	$ 572,000

Skin Care

	Current Period
Revenue	
Facial Treatments	
Standard Facials	$ 255,000
Specialty Facials	170,000
Total Facial Treatments	425,000
Waxing Services	
Body Hair Removal	10,000
Face Hair Removal	15,000
Total Waxing Services	25,000
Other	
Breakage	2,000
Service Charges	67,000
Other Revenue	10,000
Total Other	79,000
Total Revenue	529,000
Allowances	6,000
Net Revenue	523,000
Direct Expenses	
Payroll and Related Expenses	
Salaries and Wages	31,500
Commissions	148,000
Contract	13,500
Distributed Service Charges	53,500
Payroll Taxes and Employee Benefits	53,000
Total Payroll and Related Expenses	299,500
Other—Professional Products and Supplies	41,000
Total Direct Expenses	340,500
Departmental Contribution	$ 182,500

Hair

	Current Period
Revenue	
Color and Chemical	
Color	$ 48,000
Perms and Relaxers	9,000
Total Color and Chemical	57,000
Styling	
Extensions	8,000
Haircuts	50,000
Specialty Styling	50,000
Total Styling	108,000
Other	
Breakage	2,000
Service Charges	24,800
Other Revenue	10,000
Total Other	36,800
Total Revenue	201,800
Allowances	2,000
Net Revenue	199,800
Direct Expenses	
Payroll and Related Expenses	
Salaries and Wages	11,500
Commissions	52,800
Contract	5,000
Distributed Service Charges	19,800
Payroll Taxes and Employee Benefits	19,300
Total Payroll and Related Expenses	108,400
Other—Professional Products and Supplies	6,600
Total Direct Expenses	115,000
Departmental Contribution	$ 84,800

Nail

	Current Period
Revenue	
Manicure	
Nail Enhancements	$ 8,000
Specialty Manicure	8,000
Standard Manicure	64,000
Total Manicure	80,000
Pedicure	
Specialty Pedicure	9,000
Standard Pedicure	86,000
Total Pedicure	95,000
Other	
Breakage	2,000
Service Charges	26,000
Other Revenue	5,000
Total Other	33,000
Total Revenue	208,000
Allowances	2,000
Net Revenue	206,000
Direct Expenses	
Payroll and Related Expenses	
Salaries and Wages	12,200
Commissions	56,000
Contract	5,300
Distributed Service Charges	20,800
Payroll Taxes and Employee Benefits	21,100
Total Payroll and Related Expenses	115,400
Other—Professional Products and Supplies	10,500
Total Direct Expenses	125,900
Departmental Contribution	$ 80,100

Fitness

	Current Period
REVENUE	
Personal Training	$ 152,800
Group Exercise	20,000
Fitness Evaluations	16,000
Other Revenue	12,000
TOTAL REVENUE	200,800
ALLOWANCES	2,000
NET REVENUE	198,800
DIRECT EXPENSES	
Payroll and Related Expenses	
Salaries and Wages	66,000
Commissions	84,000
Contract	11,000
Payroll Taxes and Employee Benefits	39,900
Total Payroll and Related Expenses	200,900
Other Expenses	
Ambience	1,400
Athletic Equipment and Supplies	2,600
Contract Services	1,500
Equipment Rental	1,700
Guest Supplies	2,200
Hospitality	2,000
Laundry	3,000
Licenses and Fees	800
Linen	1,400
Operating Supplies	2,800
Professional Development	600
Telecommunications	900
Uniforms	1,000
Other	1,000
Total Other Expenses	22,900
TOTAL DIRECT EXPENSES	223,800
DEPARTMENTAL INCOME (LOSS)	$ (25,000)

Food and Beverage

	Current Period
Revenue	
Food	$ 84,000
Beverage	14,000
Other Revenue	2,000
Total Revenue	100,000
Allowances	1,000
Net Revenue	99,000
Cost of Goods Sold	
Food	28,400
Beverage	3,700
Total Cost of Sales	32,100
Gross Margin	66,900
Direct Expenses	
Expenses	
Payroll and Related Expenses	
Salaries and Wages	35,100
Payroll Taxes and Employee Benefits	9,700
Total Payroll and Related Expenses	44,800
Other Expenses	
Banquet and Party Costs	2,400
China, Glassware, Silver, and Linen	2,000
Contract Services	800
Dues and Subscriptions	400
Equipment Rental	700
Laundry	2,000
Licenses and fees	800
Operating Supplies	4,500
Professional Development	600
Telecommunications	500
Uniforms	900
Utensils	1,400
Other	1,000
Total Other Expenses	18,000
Total Direct Expenses	62,800
Departmental Income (Loss)	$ 4,100

Membership Dues and Fees

	Current Period
Revenue	
Daily Facility/Guest Fees	$ 42,000
Initiation Fees	48,000
Membership Dues	80,000
Other Revenue	5,000
Total Revenue	175,000
Allowances	1,000
Net Revenue	$ 174,000

Retail

	Current Period
Revenue	
Apparel	
Footwear	$ 5,000
Men's/Unisex	31,800
Robes and Terry	32,000
Women's	90,200
Total Apparel	159,000
Gifts and Accessories	
Books and Media	12,900
Fashion Accessories	43,000
Home	30,100
Total Gifts and Accessories	86,000
Products	
Bath and Body Products	72,500
Hair Products	17,500
Make-up Products	13,000
Nail Products	8,000
Private Label Products	34,000
Skin Care Products	145,000
Total Products	290,000
Other Retail	
Snacks and Beverages	22,000
Sundries	10,000
Other	8,000
Total Other Retail	40,000
Total Revenue	575,000
Revenue Adjustments	
Employee Discounts	43,000
Merchandise Returns	14,400
Allowances	2,000
Total Revenue Adjustments	59,400

(continued)

Retail *(continued)*

Net Revenue	515,600
Cost of Goods Sold	268,000
Gross Margin	247,600
Direct Expenses	
Payroll and Related Expenses	
Salaries and Wages	72,100
Commissions	13,000
Payroll Taxes and Employee Benefits	23,500
Total Payroll and Related Expenses	108,600
Other Expenses	
Buying Trips	6,000
Contract Services	500
Gift Wrap and Packaging	4,500
Licenses and Fees	500
Merchandise Displays and Accessories	2,500
Merchandise Tags	1,000
Operating Supplies	3,000
Packaging and Freight	2,000
Professional Development	600
Telecommunications	900
Uniforms	700
Other Retail Expenses	500
Total Other Expenses	22,700
Total Direct Expenses	131,300
Departmental Income (Loss)	$ 116,300

Rentals and Other Income

	Current Period
Cash Discounts Earned	$ 1,500
Cancellation and Unredeemed Gift Certificates	55,000
Interest Income	2,000
Total Rentals and Other Income	$ 58,500

Support Labor

	Current Period
SALARIES AND WAGES	
Guest Reception	$ 50,900
Host(ess)/Attendant	49,300
Housekeeping	14,500
Reservations	30,600
Supervision	48,000
Distributed Service Charges	9,600
Payroll Taxes and Employee Benefits	69,500
TOTAL SUPPORT LABOR	$ 255,200

Indirect Operating Expenses

	Current Period
Ambience	$ 7,100
Contract Services	35,200
Dues and Subscriptions	2,100
Equipment Rental	1,400
Guest Clothing	7,500
Guest Supplies	30,500
Hospitality	9,400
Laundry	43,100
Licenses and Fees	1,100
Linen	19,600
Operating Supplies	19,900
Professional Development	6,200
Telecommunications	2,200
Uniforms	2,700
Other	2,000
TOTAL INDIRECT OPERATING EXPENSES	$ 190,000

Administrative and General

	Current Period
Payroll and Related Expenses	
Management Salaries	$ 80,000
Payroll Taxes and Employee Benefits	21,300
Total Payroll and Related Expenses	101,300
Accounting Expenses	
Audit and Other External Expenses	3,600
Payroll Processing Expenses	3,000
Other Accounting Expenses	2,400
Total Accounting Expenses	9,000
Other Expenses	
Bank Charges	1,000
Cash Over/Short	(200)
Credit and Collection	2,000
Credit Card Commissions	19,000
Donations	1,000
Dues and Subscriptions	3,000
Human Resources	6,300
Information Systems	7,000
Legal and Professional	2,000
Licenses and Fees	600
Loss and Damage	500
Meals and Entertainment	1,000
Operating Supplies	2,400
Postage	600
Professional Development	700
Provision for Doubtful Accounts	3,000
Security	2,400
Telecommunications	1,300
Travel	1,700
Other	1,000
Total Other Expenses	56,300
Total Administrative and General Expenses	$ 166,600

Marketing

	Current Period
Payroll and Related Expenses	
Salaries and Wages	$ 27,000
Payroll Taxes and Employee Benefits	7,200
Total Payroll and Related Expenses	34,200
Other Expenses	
Advertising Broadcast	13,000
Advertising Print	20,000
Collateral Materials	8,700
Complimentary Guests	3,000
Direct Mail	4,500
Dues and Subscriptions	1,000
In-House Promotions	2,500
Meals and Entertainment	2,400
Postage	500
Professional Development	700
Special Events	4,000
Telecommunications	600
Trade Shows	2,400
Travel	1,000
Other Marketing	600
Total Other Expenses	64,900
Total Marketing Expenses	$ 99,100

Facility Maintenance and Utilities

	Current Period
Facility Maintenance Expenses	
Building	$ 18,000
Contract Services	3,600
Equipment Rental	500
Equipment Repair	10,000
Grounds and Landscaping	3,200
Heating, Ventilating, and Air Conditioning	2,100
Locks and Keys	2,800
Operating Supplies	8,000
Sauna, Steam, and Pool Supplies and Repairs	6,500
Trash Removal	1,800
Other Repairs and Maintenance	500
Total Facility Maintenance Expenses	57,000
Utility Expenses	
Electric	46,000
Gas	14,000
Water	11,000
Total Utility Expenses	71,000
Total Facility Maintenance and Utilities Expenses	$ 128,000

Fixed Charges

	Current Period
RENT—OTHER EQUIPMENT	$ 10,000
TAXES OTHER THAN INCOME AND PAYROLL	
Real Estate Taxes	50,000
Personal Property Taxes	5,000
Total Taxes Other than Income and Payroll	55,000
INSURANCE	
Building and Improvements	20,000
Liability	4,000
Total Insurance	24,000
TOTAL FIXED CHARGES	$ 89,000
DEPRECIATION AND AMORTIZATION	
Building and Improvements	30,000
Furnishings and Equipment	50,000
Total Depreciation and Amortization	$ 80,000
INTEREST EXPENSE—MORTGAGES	$ 30,000
(GAIN) LOSS ON SALE OF PROPERTY	$ (50,000)